The Big Christmas Collection

FOR EASY GUITAR

T0052830

ISBN 978-0-7935-4723-4

HAL•LEONARD® CORPORATION

7777 W. BLUEMOUND RD. P.O. BOX 13819 MILWAUKEE, WI 53213

The Big Christmas Collection
FOR EASY GUITAR

USING THE EASY GUITAR STRUM AND PICK PATTERNS

This chart contains the suggested Strum and Pick Patterns that are referred to by number at the beginning of each song in this book.

The symbols ⊓ and ∨ in the Strum Patterns refer to down and up strokes, respectively.

The letters in the Picking Patterns indicate which right-hand finger plays which string in the pattern:

p = thumb
i = index finger
m = middle finger
a = ring finger

For example, Picking Pattern 2 is played: thumb—index—middle—ring.

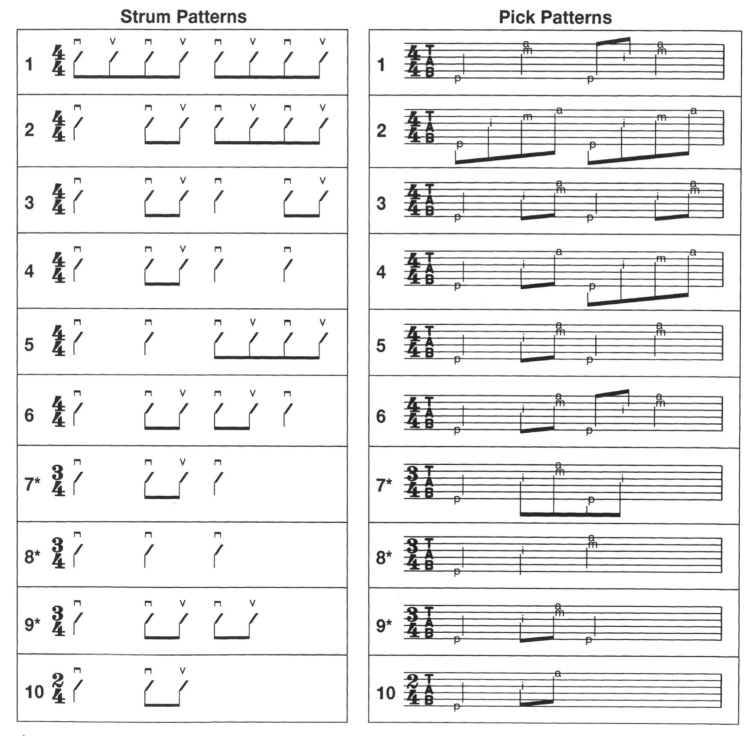

Strum Patterns   Pick Patterns

* You can use the 3/4 Strum or Pick Patterns in songs written in compound meter (6/8, 6/4, 9/8, etc.). Simply play the three-beat pattern two or more times per measure to account for the additonal beats. For example, you can accompany a song in 6/4 by playing the 3/4 pattern twice in each measure.

All My Heart This Night Rejoices

Words and Music by Johann Ebeling and Catherine Winkworth

Strum Pattern: 4
Pick Pattern: 3

Verse
Moderately

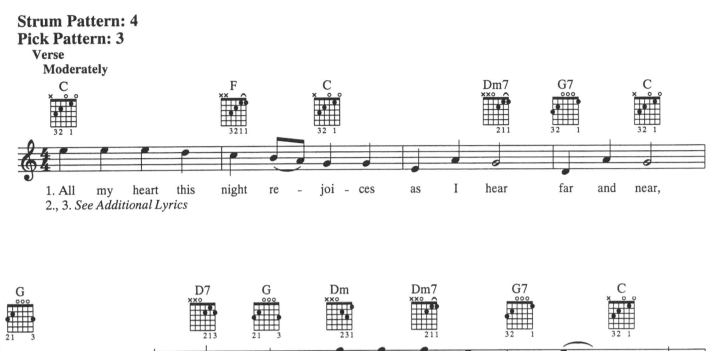

1. All my heart this night re - joi - ces as I hear far and near,
2., 3. *See Additional Lyrics*

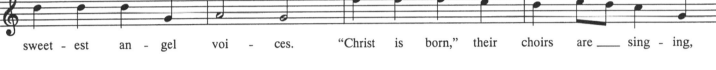

sweet - est an - gel voi - ces. "Christ is born," their choirs are ___ sing - ing,

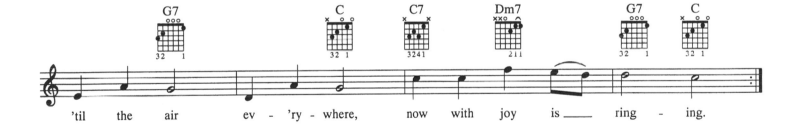

'til the air ev - 'ry - where, now with joy is ___ ring - ing.

Additional Lyrics

2. Hark! a voice from yonder manger,
   Soft and sweet doth entreat.
   "Flee from woe and danger.
   Brethren come from all that grieves you,
   You are freed.
   All you need I will surely give you."

3. Come, then, let us hasten yonder.
   Here let all, great and small,
   Kneel in awe and wonder.
   Love him who hath love is yearning.
   Hail the star that from far
   Bright with hope is burning!

All Through The Night

Traditional

Strum Pattern: 4
Pick Pattern: 3

Verse
Moderately Slow

1. Sleep, my child, and peace at-tend thee, All through the night.
2., 3. *See Additional Lyrics*

Guard - ian an - gels God will send thee, All through the night.

Soft, the drow - sy hours are creep - ing, Hill and vale in slum - ber sleep - ing.

God, his lov - ing vig - il keep - ing, All through the night.

Additional Lyrics

2. While the moon, her watch is keeping,
   All through the night.
   While the weary world is sleeping,
   All through the night.
   Through your dreams you're swiftly stealing,
   Visions of delight revealing,
   Christmas time is so appealing,
   All through the night.

3. You, my God, a babe of wonder,
   All through the night.
   Dreams you can't break from thunder,
   All through the night.
   Children's dreams cannot be broken.
   Life is but a lovely token.
   Christmas should be softly spoken,
   All through the night.

Angels We Have Heard On High

Traditional

Strum Pattern: 6
Pick Pattern: 6

Verse
Moderately

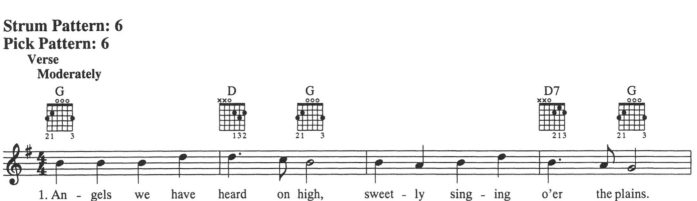

1. An - gels we have heard on high, sweet - ly sing - ing o'er the plains.
2. *See Additional Lyrics*

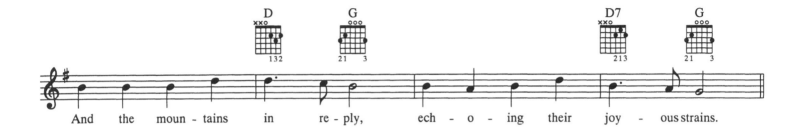

And the moun - tains in re - ply, ech - o - ing their joy - ous strains.

Chorus

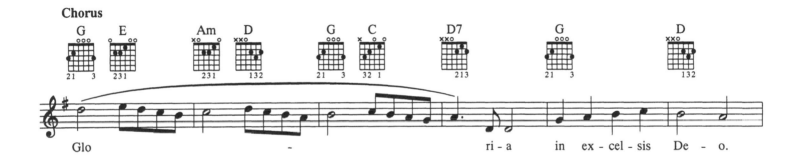

Glo - ri - a in ex - cel - sis De - o.

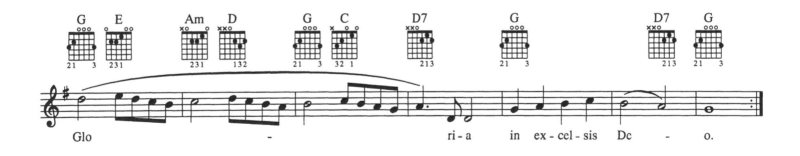

Glo - ri - a in ex - cel - sis Dc - o.

Additional Lyrics

2. Shepherds why this jubilee,
   Why your joyous strains prolong?
   What the gladsome tidings be
   Which inspire your heavenly song?

As With Gladness Men Of Old

Words by William C. Dix
Music by Conrad Kocher

Strum Pattern: 4
Pick Pattern: 5

Verse
Brightly

1. As with __ glad - ness men of old did the guid - ing star be - hold;
2., 3., 4. *See Additional Lyrics*

As with __ joy they hailed its light, lead - ing on - ward, beam - ing bright;

So, most gra - cious Lord, may we ev - er - more be led to Thee.

Additional Lyrics

2. As with joyful steps they sped,
   To that lowly manger bed,
   There to bend the knee before
   Him who Heaven and Earth adore,
   So may we with willing feet
   Ever seek thy mercy seat.

3. As they offered gifts most rare
   At that manger rude and bare,
   So may we with holy joy,
   Pure and free from sin's alloy,
   All our costliest treasures bring,
   Christ, to Thee, our heavenly King.

4. Holy Jesus, every day
   Keep us in the narrow way;
   And, when earthly things are past,
   Bring our ransomed souls at last
   Where they need no star to guide,
   Where no clouds Thy glory hide.

At The Hour Of Midnight

Traditional

Strum Pattern: 4
Pick Pattern: 5

Additional Lyrics

2. Heaven's King eternal on the straw is lying.
   Mule and ox stand near Him; from the cold He's crying.
   Spreading hay to warm Him, ox o'er Jesus hovers;
   But the mule is wicked—he the Babe uncovers.

3. Mary weeps in pity for her suff'ring darling,
   Wishing for protection from the cold winds howling.
   "Tend'rest little Savior, O my Jesus,
   All my love forever, sweetest Son so precious."

Auld Lang Syne

Words by Robert Burns
Traditional Melody

Strum Pattern: 3
Pick Pattern: 3

Verse
Moderately

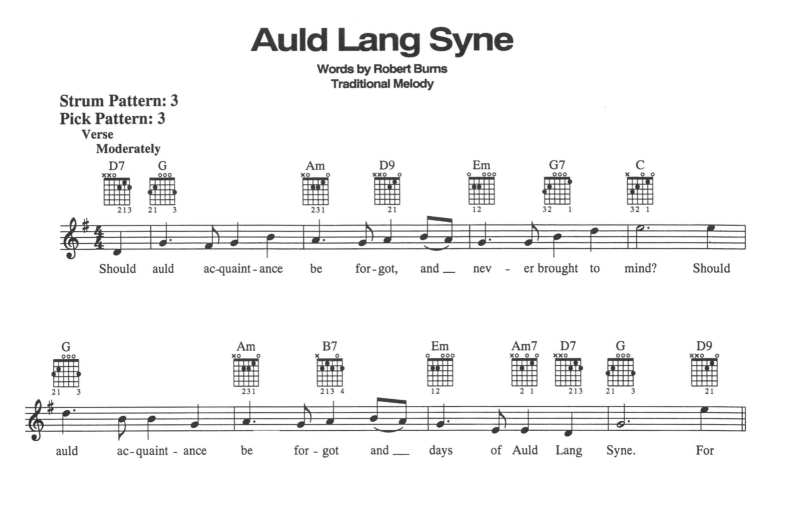

Should auld ac-quaint-ance be for-got, and __ nev - er brought to mind? Should

auld ac-quaint-ance be for - got and __ days of Auld Lang Syne. For

Chorus

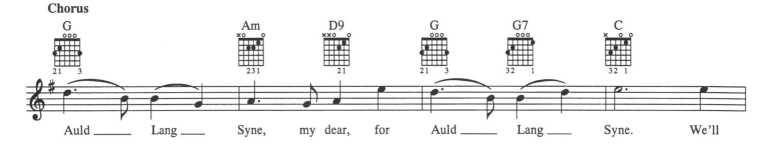

Auld ____ Lang ____ Syne, my dear, for Auld ____ Lang ____ Syne. We'll

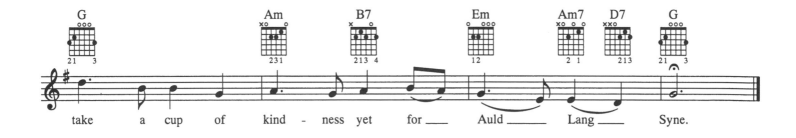

take a cup of kind - ness yet for __ Auld ____ Lang ____ Syne.

Ave Maria

By Franz Schubert

Strum Pattern: 1
Pick Pattern: 2

Verse
Reverently

G Em G D7 Em Am D7

1. A - ve Ma - ri - a! Gra - ti - a ___ ple -
2. A - ve Ma - ri - a! Ma - ter ___ De -

G Em F# D#°7

na, Ma - ri - a gra - ti - a ple - na, Ma - ri - a gra - ti - a ___ ple -
i, O - ra pro no - bis pec - ca - to - ri - bus, O - ra o - ra pro no -

Em D E7 D A7 D

na, A - ve, ___ A - ve! Do - mi - nus, ___ Do - mi - nus te - cum, Be - ne -
bis, O - ra, ra ___ pro no - bis ___ pec - ca - to - ri - bus, No - ne

D7 G D Em

dic - ta tu in mu - li - e - re-bus et be - ne - dic - tus, et
et in ho - ra ___ mor - tis, in ho - ra mor - tis no - strae, in

D B Am E°7 D D7

be - ne - dic - tus, fruc - tus ven - tris, ven - tris tu - i, Je - sus.
ho - ra mor - tis, mor - tis no - strae, in ___ ho - ra mor - tis no - strae.

G Em G D7 G G7 C Cm G

A - ve Ma - ri - a!
A - ve Ma - ri - a!

Away In A Manger

Words by Martin Luther
Music by Jonathan E. Spillman

Strum Pattern: 9
Pick Pattern: 7

Verse
Sweetly

The Birthday Of A King

Text is Anonymous
Music by William Neidlinger

Strum Pattern: 4
Pick Pattern: 3

Verse
Slowly

1. In the lit - tle vil-lage of Beth - le - hem, there lay a child one day. And the
2. *See Additional Lyrics*

sky was bright with a ho - ly light o'er the place where Je - sus lay. Al - le -

Chorus

lu - ia, oh, how the an - gels sang! Al - le - lu - ia, how it rang! And the sky was bright with a

ho - ly light; 'twas the birth - day of a king! 2. 'Twas a

Additional Lyrics

2. 'Twas a humble birthplace
   But oh, how much God gave us that day!
   From the manger bed, what a path has led,
   What a perfect holy way.

Blue Christmas

Words and Music by Billy Hayes and Jay Johnson

Bring A Torch, Jeanette, Isabella

Traditional

Strum Pattern: 8, 9
Pick Pattern: 8, 7

Verse
Brightly

1. Bring a torch, _____ Jean-ette, Is-a-bel-la;
2. *See Additional Lyrics*

bring a torch, _____ come swift-ly and run.

Christ is born, tell the folk of the vil-lage,

Je-sus is sleep-ing in His cra-dle. Ah,

ah, beau-ti-ful is the Moth-er. Ah,

ah, beau-ti-ful is her Son. _____

Additional Lyrics

2. Hasten now, good folk of the village,
Hasten now, the Christ Child to see.
You will find him asleep in a manger,
Quitely come and whisper softly.
Hush, hush, peacefully now he slumbers,
Hush, hush, peacefully now He sleeps.

Burgundian Carol

Words and Music by Oscar Brand

Strum Pattern: 8
Pick Pattern: 8

1. The winter season of the year, when to this world our Lord was born, the
2. *See Additional Lyrics*

ox and donkey, so they say, did keep His Holy Presence warm.

Chorus

How many oxen and donkeys now, if they were there when

first ____ He came? How many oxen and donkeys you

know at such a time would do the same? _____

Additional Lyrics

2. As soon as to these humble beasts
   Appeared our Lord, so mild and sweet,
   With joy they knelt before His grace
   And gently kissed His tiny feet.

Chorus If we, like oxen and donkeys then,
   In spite of all the things we've heard,
   Would like to be oxen and donkeys then,
   We'd hear the truth, believe His word.

Caroling, Caroling

Words by Wihla Hutson
Music by Alfred Burt

Strum Pattern: 8
Pick Pattern: 8
Verse
With A Lilt

1. Car - ol - ing, car - ol - ing, now we go; Christ-mas bells are ring - ing!
2., 3. *See Additional Lyrics*

Car - ol - ing, car - ol - ing, through the snow; Christ - mas bells are ring - ing!

Joy - ous voic - es sweet and clear, sing the sad of heart to cheer.

Ding, dong, ding, dong, Christ - mas bells are ring - ing!

Additional Lyrics

2. Caroling, caroling, through the town;
   Christmas bells are ringing!
   Caroling, caroling, up and down;
   Christmas bells are ringing!
   Mark ye well the song we sing,
   Gladsome tidings now we bring.
   Ding, dong, ding, dong,
   Christmas Bells are ringing!

3. Caroling, caroling, near and far;
   Christmas bells are ringing!
   Following, following yonder star;
   Christmas bells are ringing!
   Sing we all this happy morn,
   "Lo, the King of heav'n is born!"
   Ding, dong, ding, dong,
   Christmas bells are ringing!

The Chipmunk Song

Words and Music by Ross Bagdasarian

Strum Pattern: 8
Pick Pattern: 8

Verse
Happily

C   G7

Christ - mas, Christ - mas time is near. Time for toys and

time for cheer. We've been good but we can't last.

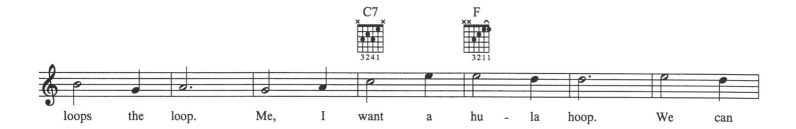

Hur - ry Christ - mas, hur - ry fast! Want a plane that

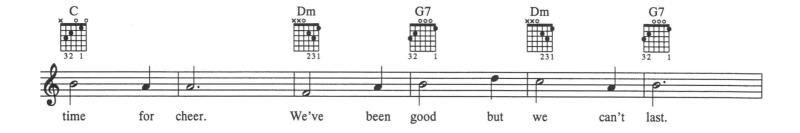

loops the loop. Me, I want a hu - la hoop. We can

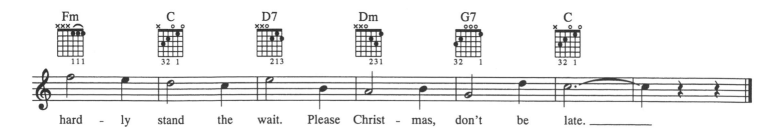

hard - ly stand the wait. Please Christ - mas, don't be late. _____

C-H-R-I-S-T-M-A-S

Words by Jenny Lou Carson
Music by Eddy Arnold

Strum Pattern: 3
Pick Pattern: 3

Verse
Brightly

The Christmas Song
(Chestnuts Roasting On An Open Fire)

Music and Lyric by Mel Torme and Robert Wells

Strum Pattern: 2
Pick Pattern: 3

Verse
Sentimentally

so I'm of-fer-ing this sim-ple phrase to kids from one to nine-ty-two. Al-

though it's been said man-y times, man-y ways, "Mer-ry Christ-mas to you."

Hear Them Bells

Words and Music by D.S. McCosh

Strum Pattern: 3
Pick Pattern: 3

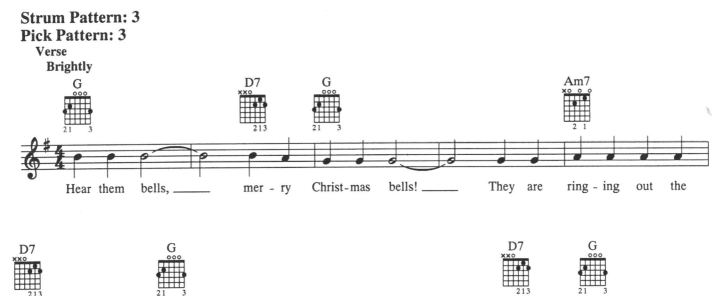

Verse
Brightly

Hear them bells, _____ mer-ry Christ-mas bells! _____ They are ring-ing out the

e-vil of the sword. _____ Hear them bells, _____ mer-ry Christ-mas bells! _

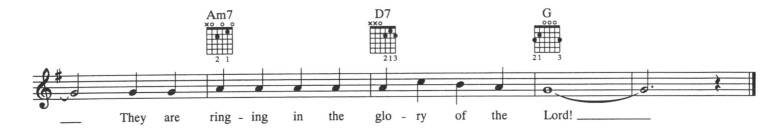

_____ They are ring-ing in the glo-ry of the Lord! _____

The Christmas Waltz

Words by Sammy Cahn
Music by Jule Styne

Strum Pattern: 9
Pick Pattern: 7

Verse
Moderately, With Expression

Come, Thou Long-Expected Jesus

Words by Charles Wesley
Music by Rowland Hugh Prichard

Strum Pattern: 8, 7
Pick Pattern: 8, 7

Verse
Moderately

Additional Lyrics

2. Born thy people to deliver,
   Born a child and yet a king.
   Born to reign in us forever,
   Now thy gracious kingdom bring.
   By thine own eternal Spirit,
   Rule in all our hearts alone.
   By thine all-sufficient merit,
   Raise us to thy glorious throne.

Deck The Hall

Traditional

Strum Pattern: 4, 6
Pick Pattern: 5, 6

Verse
Gaily

1. Deck the hall with boughs of hol - ly; fa, la, la, la, la, la, la, la, la.
2., 3. *See Additional Lyrics*

'Tis the sea - son to be jol - ly; fa, la, la, la, la, la, la, la, la.

Don we now our gay ap - par - el; fa, la, la, la, la, la, la, la, la.

Troll the an - cient yule - tide car - ol; fa, la, la, la, la, la, la, la, la.

Additional Lyrics

2. See the blazing yule before us;
   Fa, la, la, la, la, la, la, la, la.
   Strike the harp and join the chorus;
   Fa, la, la, la, la, la, la, la, la.
   Follow me in merry measure;
   Fa, la, la, la, la, la, la, la, la.
   While I tell of Yuletide treasure;
   Fa, la, la, la, la, la, la, la, la.

3. Fast away the old year passes;
   Fa, la, la, la, la, la, la, la, la.
   Hail the new ye lads and lasses;
   Fa, la, la, la, la, la, la, la, la.
   Sing we joyous, all together;
   Fa, la, la, la, la, la, la, la, la.
   Heedless of the wind and weather;
   Fa, la, la, la, la, la, la, la, la.

Do They Know It's Christmas?

Words and Music by M. Ure and B. Geldof

Strum Pattern: 3, 4
Pick Pattern: 3, 4
Verse
Medium Rock In Two

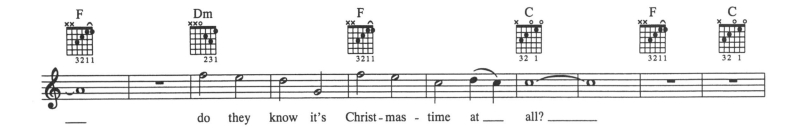

____ do they know it's Christ-mas - time at ___ all? _____

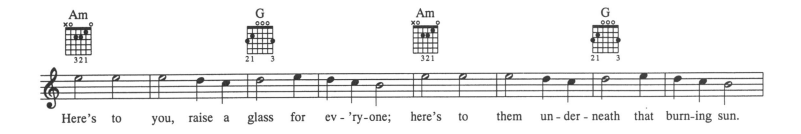

Here's to you, raise a glass for ev - 'ry-one; here's to them un - der - neath that burn-ing sun.

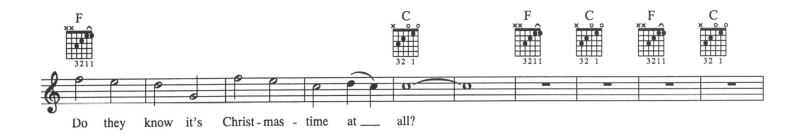

Do they know it's Christ-mas - time at ___ all?

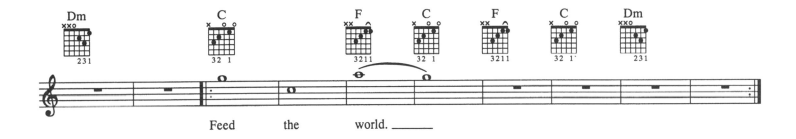

Feed the world. _____

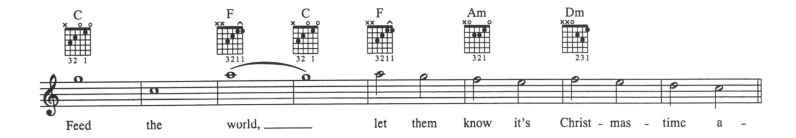

Feed the world, _____ let them know it's Christ - mas - time a –

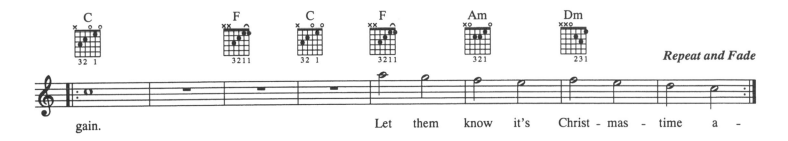

Repeat and Fade

gain. Let them know it's Christ - mas - time a –

Feliz Navidad

Words and Music by Jose Feliciano

Strum Pattern: 2, 1
Pick Pattern: 4, 2

The First Noel

Traditional

Strum Pattern: 7, 8
Pick Pattern: 9, 8

Verse
Moderately Slow

1. The __ first __ No - ël, the __ an - gel did say, was to cer - tain poor
2.-5. *See Additional Lyrics*

shep - herds in fields as they lay. In __ fields __ where _ they lay __ keep - ing their

sheep, on a cold win - ter's night ___ that was ___ so deep. No -

Chorus

ël, ___ No - ël, No - ël, No - ël, born is the King _ of Is - ra - el.

Additional Lyrics

2. They looked up and saw a star
   Shining in the East, beyond them far.
   And to the earth it gave great light
   And so it continued both day and night.

3. And by the light of that same star,
   Three wise man came from country far;
   To seek for a King was their intent,
   And to follow the star wherever it went.

4. This star drew nigh to the northwest,
   O'er Bethlehem it took its rest;
   And there it did both stop and stay,
   Right over the place where Jesus lay.

5. Then entered in those wise men three,
   Full reverently upon their knee;
   And offered there in His presence,
   Their gold, and myrrh, and frankincense.

The Friendly Beasts

English

Strum Pattern: 8
Pick Pattern: 9

Verse
Moderately

1. Je - sus our broth - er, kind and good, was hum - bly
2.-6. *See Additional Lyrics*

born in a sta - ble rude; and the friend - ly beasts a -

round Him stood, Je - sus our broth - er kind and good.

Additional Lyrics

2. "I," said the donkey, shaggy and brown,
   "I carried his mother up hill and down.
   I carried his mother to Bethlehem town."
   "I," said the donkey, shaggy and brown.

3. "I," said the cow, all white and red,
   "I gave Him my manger for His bed;
   I gave Him my hay to pillow His head."
   "I," said the cow, all white and red.

4. "I," said the sheep with the curly horn,
   "I gave Him my wool for His blanket warm;
   He wore my coat on Christmas morn."
   "I," said the sheep with the curly horn.

5. "I," said the dove from the rafters high,
   "I cooed Him to sleep that He would not cry;
   We cooed Him to sleep, my mate and I."
   "I," said the dove from the rafters high.

6. Thus every beast by some good spell,
   In the stable dark was glad to tell
   Of the gift he gave Emmanuel,
   The gift he gave Emmanuel.

Frosty The Snow Man

Words and Music by Steve Nelson and Jack Rollins

Strum Pattern: 3, 2
Pick Pattern: 3, 4

Verse

Frost-y the snow man was a-live as he could be, and the
Frost-y the snow man had to hur-ry on his way, and but he

chil-dren say he could laugh and play just the same as you and me.
waved good-bye say-in', "Don't you cry, I'll be back a-gain some day."

Outro

Thup-et-y thump thump, thump-et-y thump thump, look at Frost-y go.

Thump-et-y thump thump, thump-et-y thump thump, o-ver the hills of snow.

Grandma's Killer Fruitcake

Words and Music by Elmo Shropshire and Rita Abrams

Strum Pattern: 3
Pick Pattern: 5

Intro
Country Polka

1. The

Verse

hol-i-days were up-on us and things were go-in' fine, 'til the

day I heard the door - bell and a chill ran up my spine. I

grabbed the wife and chil - dren as the post - man wheeled it in. A

year - ly Christ - mas night - mare has just come back a - gain. It was

Chorus

hard - er than the head of Un - cle Buck - y, heav - y as a Ser - mon of Preach - er Luck - y.

One's e - nough to give the whole state of Ken - tuck - y a great big bel - ly - ache. It was

dens - er than a drove of barn - yard tur - keys, tough - er than a truck load of all beef jerk - y.

Dri - er than a drought in Al - bu - quer - que, Grand - ma's kil - ler fruit - cake. cake.

Additional Lyrics

2. Now I've had to swallow some marginal fare at our family feast.
I even downed Aunt Dolly's possom pie just to keep the family peace.
I winced at Wilma's gizzard mousse, but said it tasted fine,
But that lethal weapon that Grandma bakes is where I draw the line.

3. It's early Christmas morning, the phone rings us awake.
It's Grandma, Pa, she wants to know how'd we like the cake.
"Well, Grandma, I never. Uh we couldn't. It was, uh, unbelievable, that's for shore.
What's that you say? Oh, no Grandma, Puh-leez don't send us more!"

Fum, Fum, Fum

Traditional Spanish Carol

Strum Pattern: 4
Pick Pattern: 3

Additional Lyrics

2. Thanks to God for holidays, sing fum, fum, fum.
   Thanks to God for holidays, sing fum, fum, fum.
   Now we all our voices raise.
   And sing a song of grateful praise.
   Celebrate in song and story, all the wonders of his glory.
   Fum, fum, fum.

Gather Around The Christmas Tree

By John H. Hopkins

Strum Pattern: 4
Pick Pattern: 5

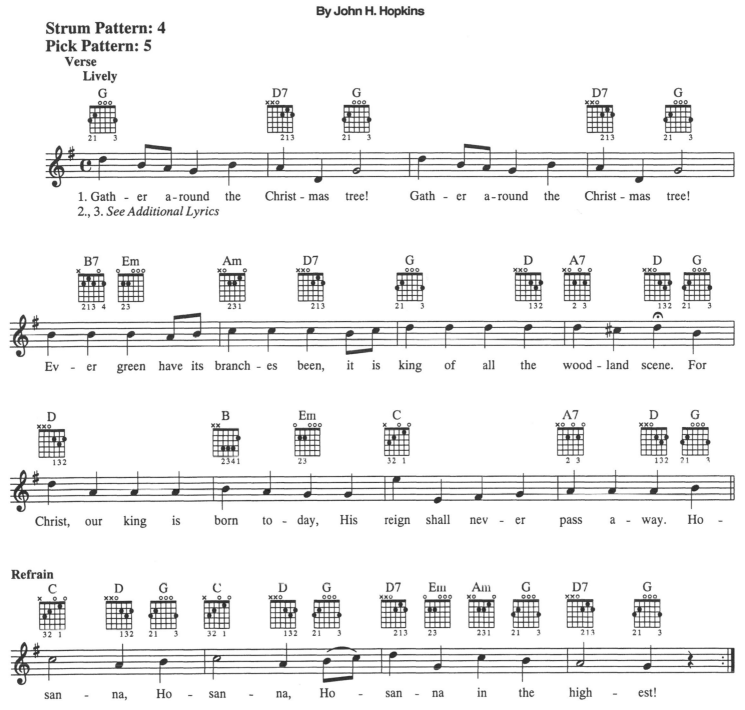

Verse
Lively

1. Gath - er a-round the Christ - mas tree! Gath - er a-round the Christ - mas tree!
2., 3. *See Additional Lyrics*

Ev - er green have its branch - es been, it is king of all the wood - land scene. For

Christ, our king is born to - day, His reign shall nev - er pass a - way. Ho -

Refrain

san - na, Ho - san - na, Ho - san - na in the high - est!

Additional Lyrics

2. Gather around the Christmas tree!
   Gather around the Christmas tree!
   Once the pride of the mountainside,
   Now cut down to grace our Christmastide.
   For Christ from heav'n to earth came down
   To gain, through death, a nobler crown.

3. Gather around the Christmas tree!
   Gather around the Christmas tree!
   Ev'ry bough has a burden now,
   They are gifts of love for us, we trow.
   For Christ is born, his love to show
   And give good gifts to men below.

Go Tell It On The Mountain

Traditional

Strum Pattern: 2, 3
Pick Pattern: 3, 4

Chorus
Moderate Swing

Go tell it on the moun - tain, o - ver the hills and ev - 'ry - where. _

Go tell it on the moun - tain, that Je - sus Christ _ is born.

Fine

Verse

1. When I was a seek - er, I sought both night and day. I
2. *See Additional Lyrics*

asked the Lord to help me, and He showed me the way. _____ all. _____

1.
2. *D.C. al Fine*

Additional Lyrics

2. He made me a watchman
Upon the city wall.
And if I am a Christian,
I am the least of all.

God Rest Ye Merry, Gentlemen

Traditional

Strum Pattern: 3, 5
Pick Pattern: 3, 4

Verse
Moderately

1. God rest ye mer - ry, gen - tle - men, let noth - ing you dis - may. For
2. *See Additional Lyrics*

Je - sus Christ our Sav - ior was born up - on this day, to

save us all from Sa - tan's power when we were gone a - stray. O ____

Chorus

tid - ings of com - fort and joy, com - fort and joy. O ____

tid - ings of com - fort and joy! 2. In joy!

Additional Lyrics

2. In Bethlehem, in Jewry
   This blessed babe was born
   And laid within a manger
   Upon this blessed morn
   To which His mother Mary
   Did nothing take in scorn.

Good Christian Men, Rejoice

Traditional

Strum Pattern: 9
Pick Pattern: 7

Verse
With Spirit

G

1. Good Chris - tian men, re - joice _____ with heart and soul and voice. _____
2. *See Additional Lyrics*

D7   G   Am7   D7

Give ye heed to what we say: Je - sus Christ is born to - day!

Em   Am7   D7   Em

Ox and ass be - fore Him bow, and He is in the man - ger now.

C   D7   G   D7   G   D7   1. G   2. G

Christ is born to - day! _____ Christ is born to - day. 2. Good this!

Additional Lyrics

2. Good Christian men, rejoice
   With heart and soul and voice.
   Now ye hear of endless bliss:
   Jesus Christ was born for this.
   He hath op'd the heavenly door,
   And man is blessed evermore.
   Christ was born for this!
   Christ was born for this!

Good King Wenceslas

Traditional

Strum Pattern: 4, 3
Pick Pattern: 5, 3

Verse
With Spirit

1. Good King Wen - ces - las looked out on the feast of Ste - phen;
2.-5. *See Additional Lyrics*

when the snow lay 'round a - bout, deep and crisp and e - ven.

Bright - ly shone the moon that night, though the frost was cru - el;

when a poor man came in sight, gath - 'ring win - ter fu - el.

Additional Lyrics

2. "Hither page, and stand by me,
   If thou know'st it, telling;
   Yonder peasant, who is he?
   Where and what his dwelling?"
   "Sire, he lives a good league hence,
   Underneath the mountain;
   Right against the forest fence,
   By Saint Agnes' fountain."

3. "Bring me flesh, and bring me wine,
   Bring me pine-logs hither;
   Thou and I will see him dine,
   When we bear them thither."
   Page and monarch forth they went,
   Forth they went together;
   Through the rude winds wild lament,
   And the bitter weather.

4. "Sire, the night is darker now,
   And the wind blows stronger;
   Fails my heart, I know not how,
   I can go not longer."
   "Mark my footsteps, my good page,
   Tread thou in them boldly:
   Thou shalt find the winter's rage
   Freeze thy blood less coldly."

5. In his master's steps he trod,
   Where the snow lay dinted;
   Heat was in the very sod
   Which the saint has printed.
   Therefore, Christian men, be sure,
   Wealth or rank possessing;
   Ye who now will bless the poor,
   Shall yourselves find blessing.

The Greatest Gift Of All

Words and Music by John Jarvis

Hard Candy Christmas

Words and Music by Carol Hall

⊕ *Coda*

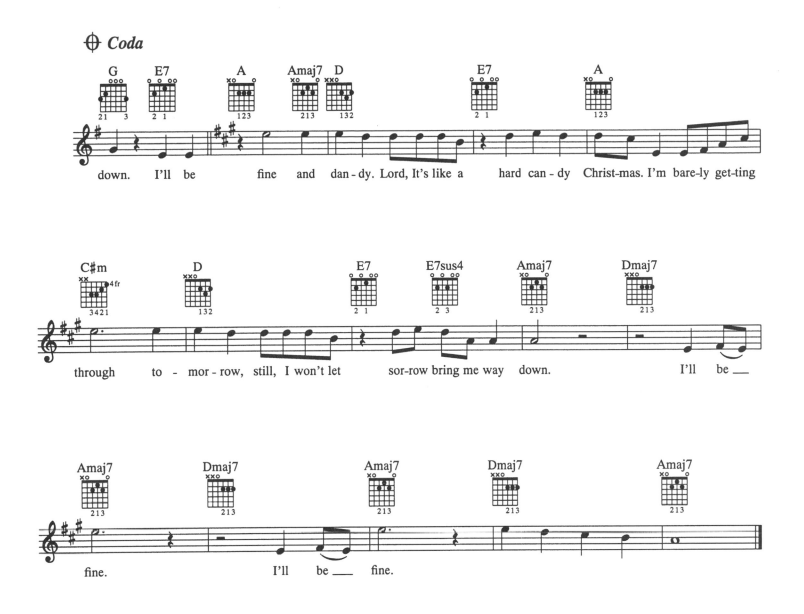

Additional Lyrics

2. Hey, maybe I'll learn to sew,
   Maybe I'll just lie low.
   Maybe I'll hit the bars,
   Maybe I'll count the stars
   Until the dawn.
   Me, I will go on.
   Maybe I'll settle down,
   Maybe I'll just leave town.
   Maybe I'll have some fun,
   Maybe I'll meet someone
   And make 'em mine.

Happy Holiday

Words and Music by Irving Berlin

Strum Pattern: 3, 2
Pick Pattern: 3, 4

Verse
Slowly

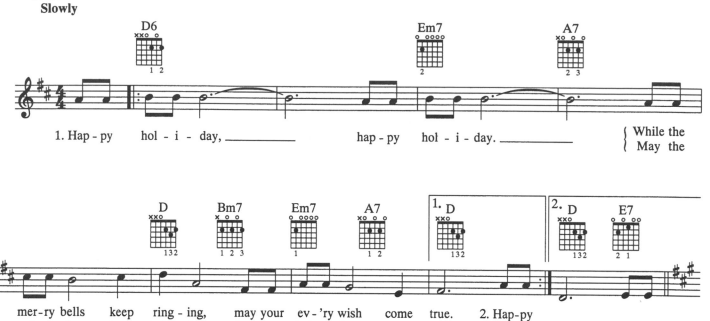

1. Hap - py hol - i - day, _____ hap - py hol - i - day. _____ { While the / May the

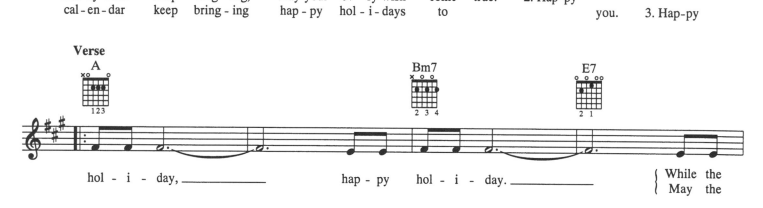

mer - ry bells keep ring - ing, may your ev - 'ry wish come true. 2. Hap-py
cal - en - dar keep bring - ing hap - py hol - i - days to you. 3. Hap-py

Verse

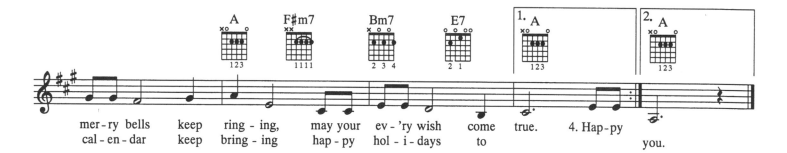

hol - i - day, _____ hap - py hol - i - day. _____ { While the / May the

mer - ry bells keep ring - ing, may your ev - 'ry wish come true. 4. Hap-py
cal - en - dar keep bring - ing hap - py hol - i - days to you.

Hark! The Herald Angels Sing

Words by Charles Wesley
Music by Felix Mendelssohn-Bartholdy

Strum Pattern: 2, 3
Pick Pattern: 3, 4

Verse
Joyfully

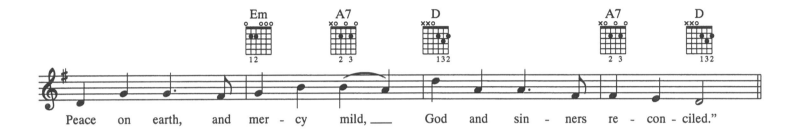

Hark! The her-ald an-gels sing, ___ "Glo-ry to the new-born King!

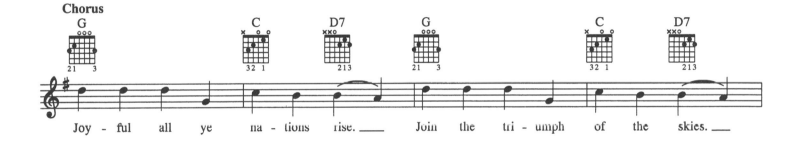

Peace on earth, and mer-cy mild, ___ God and sin-ners re-con-ciled."

Chorus

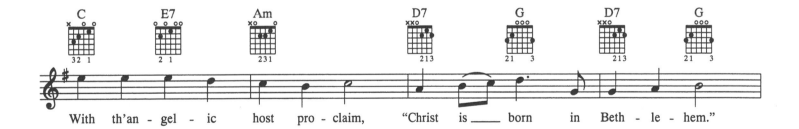

Joy-ful all ye na-tions rise. ___ Join the tri-umph of the skies. ___

With th'an-gel-ic host pro-claim, "Christ is ___ born in Beth-le-hem."

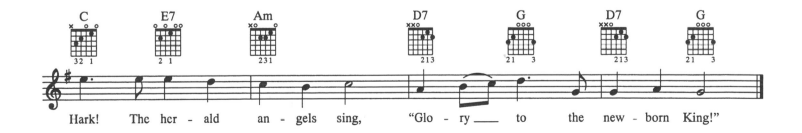

Hark! The her-ald an-gels sing, "Glo-ry ___ to the new-born King!"

He

Words Richard Mullen
Music by Jack Richards

Strum Pattern: 9
Pick Pattern: 9

Intro
Moderately Slow

1. He can turn the tides and calm the an - gry sea. He a - lone de - cides who writes a sym - pho - ny. He lights ev - 'ry star that makes our dark - ness bright. He keeps watch all through each long and lone - ly night. He still finds the time to hear a child's first prayer. Saint or sin - ner, call and al - ways find Him there.

Chorus

Though it makes him sad to see the way we live, he'll al - ways say, "I for - give." give, I for - give."

Additional Lyrics

2. He can grant a wish or make a dream come true.
He can paint the clouds and turn the gray to blue.
He alone knows where to find the rainbow's end.
He alone can see what lies beyond the bend.
He can touch a tree and turn the leaves to gold.
He knows every lie that you and I have told.

Here We Come A-Wassailing

Traditional

Strum Pattern: 7, 9
Pick Pattern: 7, 9

Strum Pattern: 3
Pick Pattern: 3

Additional Lyrics

2. We are not daily beggars
   That beg from door to door.
   But we are neighbor children
   Whom you have seen before.

3. We have got a little purse
   Of stretching leather skin.
   We want a little money
   To line it well within:

4. God bless the master of this house,
   Likewise the mistress too;
   And all the little children
   That round the table go:

A Holly Jolly Christmas

Music and Lyrics by Johnny Marks

Strum Pattern: 2, 3
Pick Pattern: 3, 4

case you did-n't hear Oh, by gol-ly, have a hol-ly jol-ly Christ-mas this

year. 1. Have a Christ-mas _____ this year. _____

O Come, Little Children

Traditional

Strum Pattern: 10
Pick Pattern: 10

Verse
Quietly

1. O come, lit-tle chil-dren, from cot and from hall, O come to the
2. *See Additional Lyrics*

man-ger in Beth-le-hem's stall. There meek-ly He li-eth, the

heav-en-ly child, so poor and so hum-ble, so sweet and so mild.

Additional Lyrics

2. Now "Glory to God!" sing the angels on high
   And "Peace upon earth!" heavenly voices reply.
   Then come little children and join in the day
   That gladdened the world on that first Christmas day.

(There's No Place Like) Home For The Holidays

Words by Al Stillman
Music by Robert Allen

Strum Pattern: 3
Pick Pattern: 3

Chorus
Moderately

Oh, there's no place like home for the hol - i - days, _____ 'cause no mat - ter how far a - way you roam, _____ when you pine for the sun - shine of a friend - ly gaze, _____ for the hol - i - days you can't beat home, sweet home.

1. I met a
2. A home that

Verse

man who lives in Ten - nes - see and he was head - in' for Penn - syl - van - ia and some
knows your joy and laugh - ter filled with mem' - ries by the score is a home you're glad to

home-made pump-kin pie. / wel-come with your heart.

From Penn-syl - van - ia folks are trav-'lin' down to Dix-ie's sun - ny / From Cal - i - for - nia to New Eng-land down to Dix-ie's sun - ny

shore; / shore; From At - lan - tic to Pa - ci - fic, gee, the traf - fic is ter - ri - fic. Oh, there's

Chorus

no place like home for the hol - i - days, _____ 'cause no mat - ter how

far a - way you roam, _____ if you want to be hap - py in a mil - lion ways, _

1.

_ for the hol - i - days you can't beat home, sweet home. _____ Oh, there's

2.

can't beat home, sweet home. _____

The Holly And The Ivy

Traditional

Strum Pattern: 8
Pick Pattern: 8

Verse
Moderately Slow

Additional Lyrics

2. The holly bears a blossom,
   As white as lily flow'r,
   And Mary bore sweet Jesus Christ,
   To be our sweet Saviour.

3. The holly bears a berry,
   As red as any blood,
   And Mary bore sweet Jesus Christ,
   To do poor sinners good.

I Heard The Bells On Christmas Day

Words by Henry Longfellow
Adapted by Johnny Marks
Music by Johnny Marks

Strum Pattern: 4
Pick Pattern: 5

Verse
Simply

1. I heard the bells on Christ-mas day, their old fa-mil-iar
2., 3., 4. *See Additional Lyrics*

car - ols play. And mild and sweet the words re - peat of

peace on earth, good will to men. 2. I will to men. 3. And will to men.

Additional Lyrics

2. I thought as now this day had come,
   The belfries of all Christendom
   Had rung so long the unbroken song
   Of peace on earth, good will to men.

3. And in despair I bowed my head;
   "There is no peace on earth," I said,
   "For hate is strong, and mocks the song
   Of peace on earth, good will to men."

4. Then pealed the bells more loud and dccp;
   "God is not dead, nor noth He sleep.
   The wrong shall fail, the right prevail
   With peace on earth good will to men."

I Saw Mommy Kissing Santa Claus

Words and Music by Tommie Connor

Strum Pattern: 2, 3
Pick Pattern: 3, 4

Verse
Moderate

I Wonder As I Wander

By John Jacob Niles

Additional Lyrics

2. When Jesus was born, it was in a cow's stall,
   With shepherds and wise men and angels and all.
   The blessings of Christmas from heaven did fall
   And the weary world woke to the Savior's call.

I'll Be Home For Christmas

Words and Music by Kim Gannon and Walter Kent

Strum Pattern: 4, 3
Pick Pattern: 4, 3

In The Field With Their Flocks Abiding

Traditional

Strum Pattern: 4
Pick Pattern: 3

Verse
Moderately

In the field with their flocks a - bid - ing, they_ lay on the dew - y ground. And_

glim - mer - ing un - der the star - light, the _ sheep lay white a - round. When the

light of the Lord streamed o'er_ them, and lo! from the heav - en a - bove, an

an - gel leaned from the glo - ry, and sang his song of love. He

sang that first sweet Christ - mas the song that shall nev - er cease,

"Glo - ry to God in the high - est, on earth good will and peace."

Infant Holy, Infant Lowly

Traditonal

Strum Pattern: 7, 9
Pick Pattern: 7, 9

Verse
Lyrically

1. In - fant Ho - ly, In - fant low - ly, for His bed a cat - tle
2. *See Additional Lyrics*

stall. Ox - en low - ing, lit - tle know - ing Christ the Babe is Lord of all. Swift are

wing - ing an - gels sing - ing, no - els ring - ing, ti - dings bring - ing: Christ the Babe is Lord of

all!

you. _____

Additional Lyrics

2. Flocks are sleeping, shepherds keeping
Vigil 'til the morning new.
Saw the glory, heard the story,
Tidings of a Gospel true.
Thus rejoicing, free from sorrow,
Praises voicing, greet the morrow:
Christ the Babe was born for you.

It Came Upon The Midnight Clear

Words by Edmund H. Sears
Music by Richard S. Willis

Strum Pattern: 8, 7
Pick Pattern: 8, 9

Verse
Quitely

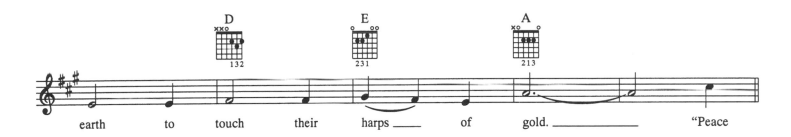

It came up - on _____ the mid - night clear, that glo - rious _____

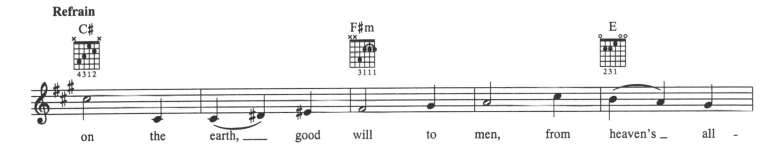

song _____ of old, _____ from an - gels bend - ing near the

earth to touch their harps _____ of gold. _____ "Peace

Refrain

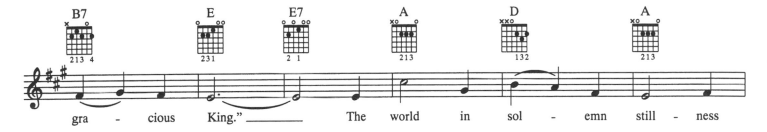

on the earth, _____ good will to men, from heaven's _ all -

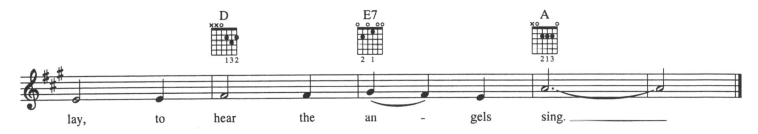

gra - cious King." _____ The world in sol - emn still - ness

lay, to hear the an - gels sing. _____

It's Beginning To Look Like Christmas

Words and Music by Meredith Willson

Strum Pattern: 2, 3
Pick Pattern: 3, 4

Verse
Brightly

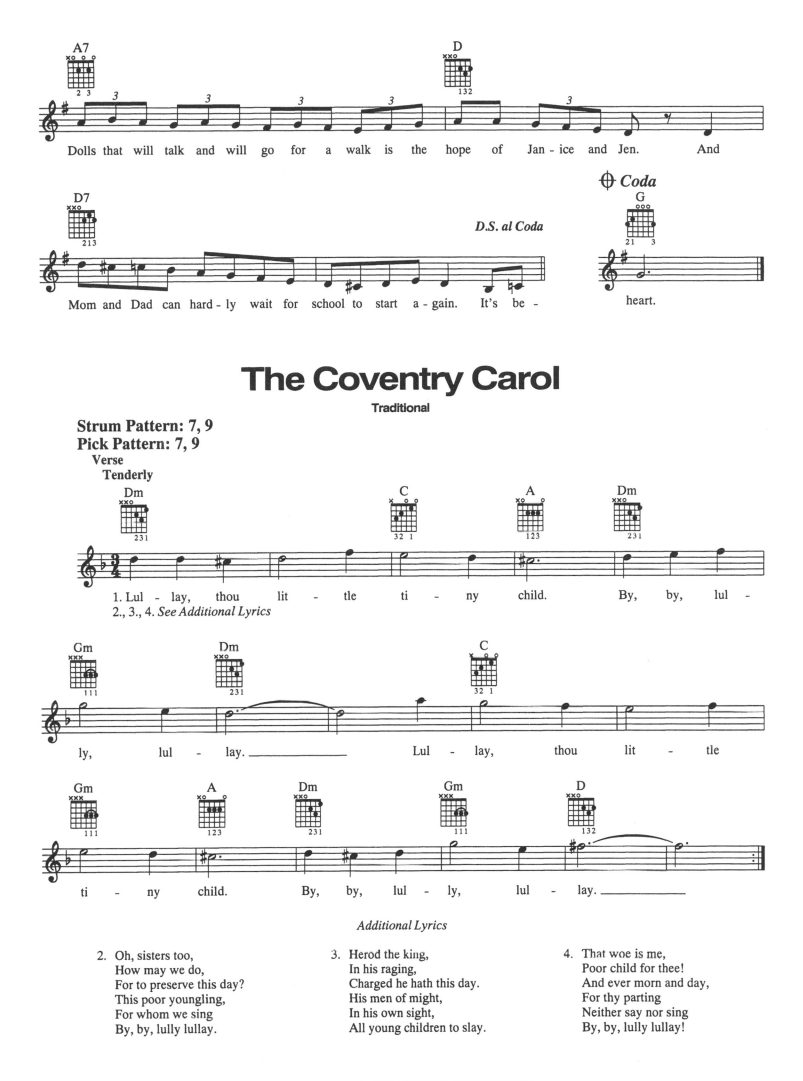

Dolls that will talk and will go for a walk is the hope of Jan - ice and Jen. And

D.S. al Coda

Mom and Dad can hard - ly wait for school to start a - gain. It's be -

⊕ *Coda*

heart.

The Coventry Carol

Traditional

Strum Pattern: 7, 9
Pick Pattern: 7, 9

Verse
Tenderly

1. Lul - lay, thou lit - tle ti - ny child. By, by, lul -
2., 3., 4. *See Additional Lyrics*

ly, lul - lay. _____ Lul - lay, thou lit - tle

ti - ny child. By, by, lul - ly, lul - lay. _____

Additional Lyrics

2. Oh, sisters too,
How may we do,
For to preserve this day?
This poor youngling,
For whom we sing
By, by, lully lullay.

3. Herod the king,
In his raging,
Charged he hath this day.
His men of might,
In his own sight,
All young children to slay.

4. That woe is me,
Poor child for thee!
And ever morn and day,
For thy parting
Neither say nor sing
By, by, lully lullay!

Jesus Holy, Born So Lowly

Traditional Polish

Strum Pattern: 8
Pick Pattern: 8

Additional Lyrics

2. On the straw the Babe is sleeping,
   In the humble manger bed.
   Mary loving watch is keeping,
   Angels hover 'round His head.
   Shepherds bow in adoration,
   Praising God's sweet benediction
   That upon the earth is shed.

Jingle Bells

Words and Music by J. Pierpont

Strum Pattern: 2, 3
Pick Pattern: 3, 4

Verse
Bright

G   C   D7

1. Dash-ing through the snow,   in a one horse o-pen sleigh.   O'er the fields we go,
2., 3. *See Additional Lyrics*

G   C

laugh-ing all the way.   Bells on bob-tail ring,   mak-ing spir-its bright.   What fun it is to

Chorus

G   D7   G   G

ride and sing a sleigh-ing song to-night! Oh! Jin-gle bells, jin-gle bells, jin-gle all the

C   G   A7   D7   G

way.   Oh, what fun it is to ride in a one horse o-pen sleigh! ___ Jin-gle bells,

C   G   D7   G

jin-gle bells, jin-gle all the way.   Oh, what fun it is to ride in a one horse o-pen sleigh!

Additional Lyrics

2. A day or two ago, I thought I'd take a ride,
   And soon Miss Fannie Bright was sitting by my side.
   The horse was lean and lank,
   Misfortune seemed his lot.
   He got into a drifted bank and we, we got upshot! Oh!

3. Now the ground is white, go it while you're young.
   Take the girls tonight and sing this sleighing song.
   Just get a bobtail bay,
   Two-forty for his speed.
   Then hitch him to an open sleigh and
   Crack, you'll take the lead! Oh

Jingle-Bell Rock

Words and Music by Joe Beal and Jim Boothe

Strum Pattern: 1, 3
Pick Pattern: 2, 3

Gid-dy-ap, jin-gle horse pick up your feet, jin-gle a-round the clock.

Mix and min-gle in a jin-gle-in' beat, that's the jin-gle-bell rock.

that's the jin-gle-bell, that's the jin-gle-bell rock. _____

While Shepherds Watched Their Flocks

Words by Nahum Tate
Music by George F. Handel

Strum Pattern: 3
Pick Pattern: 3

Verse
Moderately

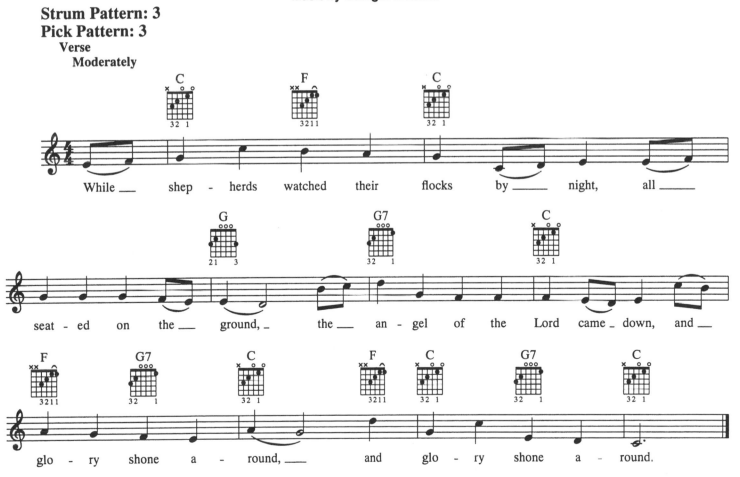

While ___ shep-herds watched their flocks by ___ night, all ___

seat-ed on the ___ ground, _ the ___ an-gel of the Lord came _ down, and ___

glo-ry shone a-round, ___ and glo-ry shone a-round.

Jolly Old St. Nicholas

Traditional

Strum Pattern: 10
Pick Pattern: 10

Verse
Brightly

1. Jol - ly old Saint Nich - o - las, lean your ear this way.
2., 3. *See Additional Lyrics*

Don't you tell a sin - gle soul what I'm going to say.

Christ - mas Eve is com - ing soon, now, you dear old man,

whis - per what you'll bring to me; tell me if you can.

Additional Lyrics

2. When the clock is striking twelve, when I'm fast asleep.
   Down the chimney broad and black, with your pack you'll creep.
   All the stockings you will find hanging in a row.
   Mine will be the shortest one, you'll be sure to know.

3. Johnny wants a pair of skates; Susy wants a sled.
   Nellie wants a picture book, yellow, blue and red.
   Now I think I'll leave to you what to give the rest.
   Choose for me, dear Santa Claus.
   You will know the best.

Joy To The World

Words by Isaac Watts
Music by George F. Handel

Strum Pattern: 3
Pick Pattern: 3
Verse
With Spirit

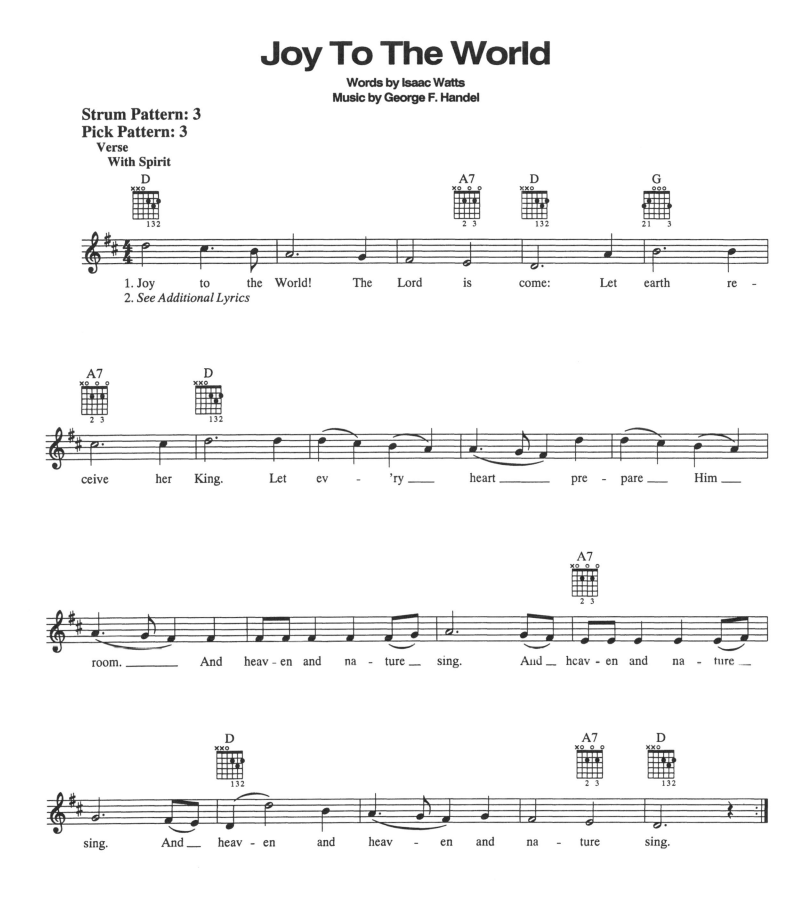

1. Joy to the World! The Lord is come: Let earth re-
2. *See Additional Lyrics*

ceive her King. Let ev - 'ry ___ heart ___ pre - pare ___ Him ___

room. ___ And heav - en and na - ture ___ sing. And ___ heav - en and na - ture ___

sing. And ___ heav - en and heav - en and na - ture sing.

Additional Lyrics

2. He rules the world with truth and grace
And makes the nations prove
The glories of His righteousness
And wonders of His love,
And wonders of His love.
And wonders, wonders of His love.

Let It Snow! Let It Snow! Let It Snow!

Words by Sammy Cahn
Music by Jule Styne

Strum Pattern: 2
Pick Pattern: 4

Lo, How A Rose E'er Blooming

Old German Hymn Tune

Strum Pattern: 3, 4
Pick Pattern: 4, 5

Verse
Hymn

1. Lo, how a ros e'er bloom - ing from ten - der stem ___
2. *See Additional Lyrics*

___ hath sprung! Of Jes - se's lin - eage com - ing, as men of old ___

___ have sung. It came, a flow'r - et bright, a - mid the

cold of win - ter, when half spent was ___ the night. ___ the night.

Additional Lyrics

2. Isaiah 'twas foretold it,
   The rose I have in mind.
   With Mary we behold it,
   The Virgin Mother kind.
   To show God's love aright.
   She bore to men a Savior
   When half spent was the night.

A Marshmallow World

Words by Carl Sigman
Music by Peter De Rose

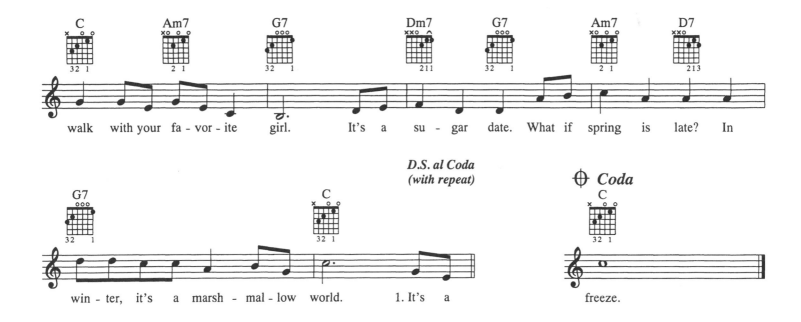

walk with your fa - vor - ite girl. It's a su - gar date. What if spring is late? In

D.S. al Coda
(with repeat)

⊕ *Coda*

win - ter, it's a marsh - mal - low world. 1. It's a

freeze.

Angels From The Realms Of Glory

Words by James Montgomery
Music by Henry Smart

Strum Pattern: 3
Pick Pattern: 5

Verse
Joyfully

1. An - gels from the realms of glo - ry, wing your flight o'er all the earth.
2. *(See Additional Lyrics)*

Ye who sang cre - a - tion's sto - ry, now pro - claim Mes - si - ah's birth.

Chorus

Come and wor - ship! Come and wor - ship! Wor - ship Christ the new - born King!

Additional Lyrics

2. Sages leave your contemplations,
   Brighter visions beam afar.
   Seek the great Desire of nations,
   Ye have seen His natal star.

March Of The Three Kings

Traditional French

Strum Pattern: 10
Pick Pattern: 10

The Marvelous Toy

Words and Music by Tom Paxton

Strum Pattern: 3
Pick Pattern: 5

Additional Lyrics

2. The first time that I picked it up, I had a big surprise,
   For right on its bottom were two big buttons
   That looked like big green eyes.
   I first pushed one and then the other, and then I twisted its lid,
   And when I set it down again, here is what it did:

3. It first marched left and then marched right
   And then marched under a chair,
   And when I looked where it had gone, it wasn't even there!
   I started to sob and my daddy laughed,
   For he knew that I would find
   When I turned around my marvelous toy, chugging from behind.

4. Well, the years have gone by too quickly, it seems,
   And I have my own little boy.
   And yesterday I gave to him my marvelous little toy.
   His eyes nearly popped right out of his head,
   And he gave a squeal of glee.
   Neither one of us knows just what it is, but he loves it, just like me.

Final Chorus:
   It still goes "zip" when it moves, and "bop" when it stops,
   And "whirr" when it stands still.
   I never knew just what it was,
   And I guess I never will.

The Most Wonderful Time Of The Year

Words and Music by Eddie Pola and George Wyle

Strum Pattern: 7
Pick Pattern: 8

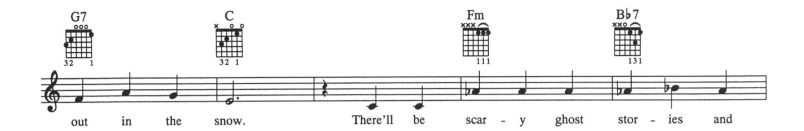

out in the snow. There'll be scar - y ghost stor - ies and

D.S. al Coda

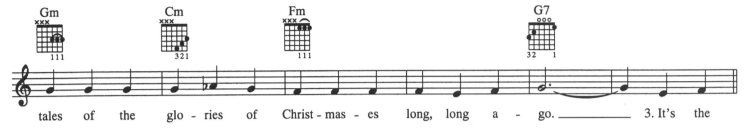

tales of the glo - ries of Christ - mas - es long, long a - go. _____ 3. It's the

⊕ *Coda*

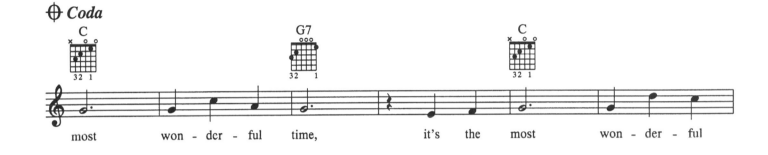

most won - der - ful time, it's the most won - der - ful

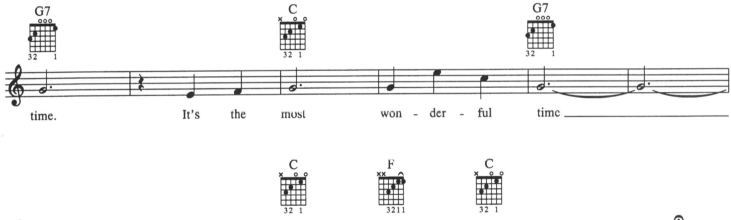

time. It's the most won - der - ful time _____

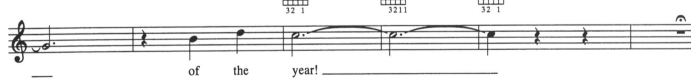

___ of the year! _____

Additional Lyrics

2. It's the hap-happiest season of all,
With those holiday greetings
And gay happy meetings
When friends come to call.
It's the hap-happiest season of all.

3. It's the most wonderful time of the year.
There'll be much mistletoeing
And hearts will be glowing
When loved ones are near.
It's the most wonderful time of the year.

Mary Had A Baby

Traditional

Strum Pattern: 1, 3
Pick Pattern: 1, 3

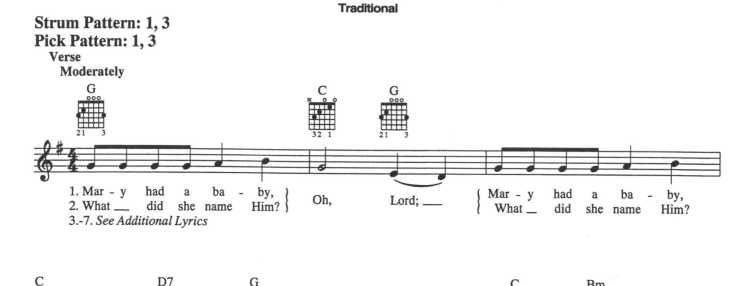

1. Mar - y had a ba - by,
2. What __ did she name Him?
3.-7. *See Additional Lyrics*

Oh, Lord; __ Mar - y had a ba - by, What __ did she name Him?

Oh, my __ Lord; Mar - y had a ba - by, What __ did she name Him? Oh, Lord; __ The

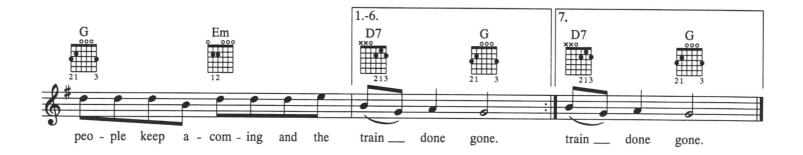

peo - ple keep a - com - ing and the train __ done gone. train __ done gone.

Additional Lyrics

3. She called Him Jesus,
4. Where was He born?
5. Born in a stable,
6. Where did they lay Him?
7. Laid Him in a manger,

My Favorite Things

Lyrics by Oscar Hammerstein II
Music by Richard Rodgers

Bridge

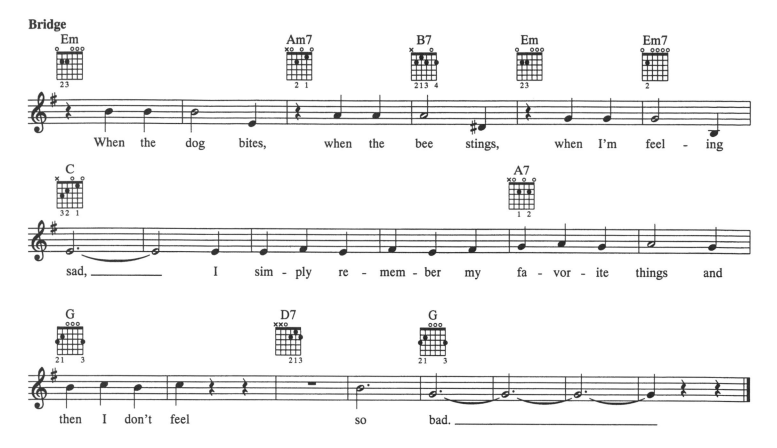

When the dog bites, when the bee stings, when I'm feel - ing

sad, ___ I sim - ply re - mem - ber my fa - vor - ite things and

then I don't feel so bad. ___

Additional Lyrics

2. Cream colored ponies and crisp apple strudles,
   Doorbells and sleigh bells and schnitzel with noodles,
   Wild geese that fly with the moon on their wings,
   These are a few of my favorite things.

Nuttin' For Christmas

Words and Music by Roy Bennett and Sid Tepper

Strum Pattern: 4
Pick Pattern: 5

Verse
Brightly

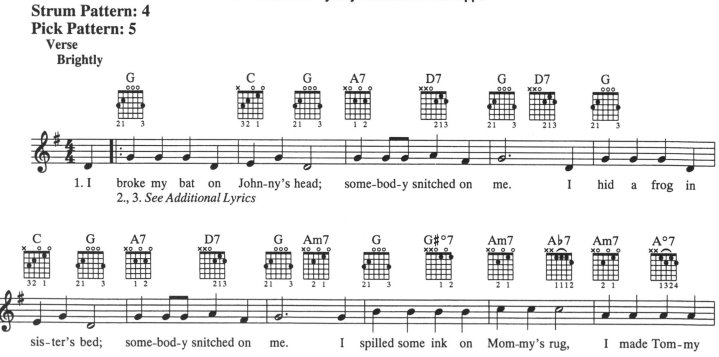

1. I broke my bat on John-ny's head; some-bod-y snitched on me. I hid a frog in
2., 3. See Additional Lyrics

sis-ter's bed; some-bod-y snitched on me. I spilled some ink on Mom-my's rug, I made Tom-my

Additional Lyrics

2. I put a tack on teacher's chair;
   Somebody snitched on me.
   I tied a knot in Susie's hair;
   Somebody snitched on me.
   I did a dance on Mommy's plants,
   Climbed a tree and tore my pants.
   Filled the sugar bowl with ants;
   Somebody snitched on me.

3. I won't be seeing Santa Claus;
   Somebody snitched on me.
   He won't come visit me because
   Somebody snitched on me.
   Next year, I'll be going straight.
   Next year, I'll be good, just wait.
   I'd start now but it's too late;
   Somebody snitched on me, Oh,

The Night Before Christmas Song

Music by Johnny Marks
Lyrics adapted by Johnny Marks from Clement Moore's Poem

Strum Pattern: 8
Pick Pattern: 8

Verse
Brightly

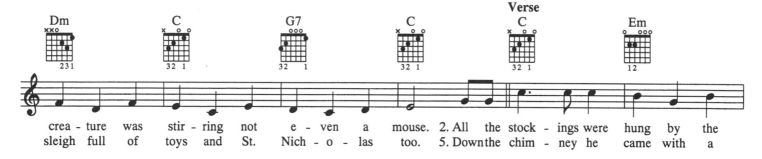

1. 'Twas the night be-fore Christ-mas and all through the house, not a
up to the house-top the rein-deer soon flew, with the

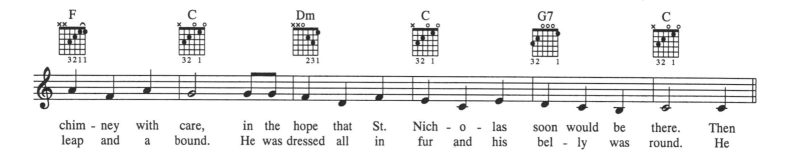

crea-ture was stir-ring not e-ven a mouse. 2. All the stock-ings were hung by the
sleigh full of toys and St. Nich-o-las too. 5. Down the chim-ney he came with a

chim-ney with care, in the hope that St. Nich-o-las soon would be there. Then
leap and a bound. He was dressed all in fur and his bel-ly was round. He

Bridge

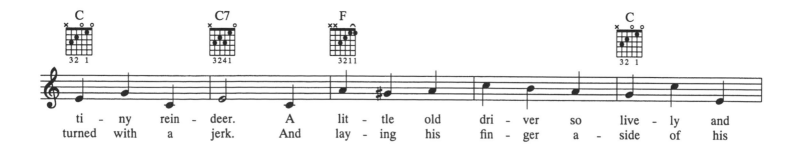

what to my won-der-ing eyes should ap-pear, a min-i-a-ture sleigh and eight
spoke not a word but went straight to his work and filled all the stock-ings; then

ti-ny rein-deer. A lit-tle old dri-ver so live-ly and
turned with a jerk. And lay-ing his fin-ger a-side of his

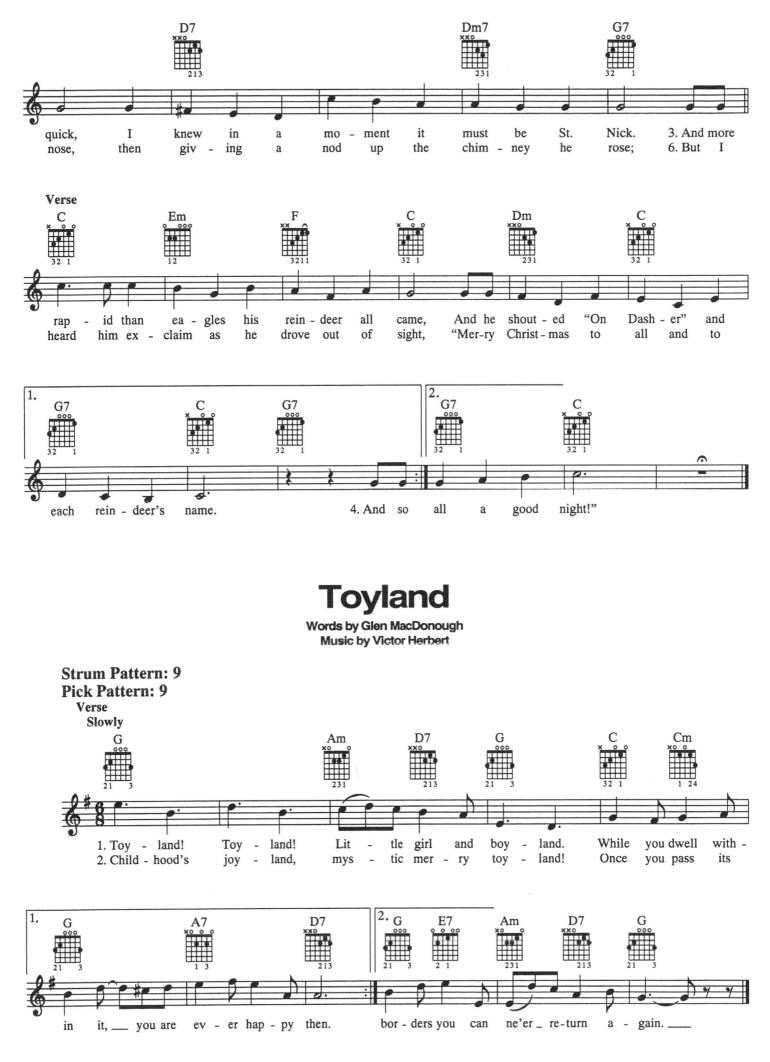

Toyland

Words by Glen MacDonough
Music by Victor Herbert

Strum Pattern: 9
Pick Pattern: 9

O Christmas Tree

Traditional

Strum Pattern: 8, 7
Pick Pattern: 8, 9

Verse
Moderately

1. O Christ-mas tree! O Christ-mas tree, you stand in ver - dant beau - ty! O
2., 3. *See Additional Lyrics*

Christ-mas tree, O Christ-mas tree, you stand in ver - dant beau - ty! Your

boughs are green in sum-mer's glow, and do not fade in win-ter's snow. O

Christ - mas tree, O Christ - mas tree, you stand in ver - dant beau - ty!

Additional Lyrics

2. O, Christmas tree! O, Christmas tree,
   Much pleasure doth thou bring me!
   O, Christmas tree! O, Christmas tree,
   Much pleasure does thou bring me!
   For every year the Christmas tree
   Brings to us all both joy and glee.
   O, Christmas tree, O, Christmas tree,
   Much pleasure doth thou bring me!

3. O, Christmas tree! O, Christmas tree,
   Thy candles shine out brightly!
   O, Christmas Tree, O, Christmas tree,
   Thy candles shine out brightly!
   Each bough doth hold its tiny light
   That makes each toy to sparkle bright.
   O, Christmas tree, O Christmas tree,
   Thy candles shine out brightly.

O Come, All Ye Faithful
(Adeste Fidelis)

Words and Music by John Francis Wade
Latin Words translated by Frederick Oakeley

Strum Pattern: 4
Pick Pattern: 5

Verse
Triumphantly

1. O Come, all ye faith - ful, joy - ful and tri - um - phant. O
2. *See Additional Lyrics*

come ye, O come ___ ye to Beth - le - hem;

Come and be - hold him, born the King of an - gels; O

Chorus

come, let us a - dore him. O come, let us a - dore him. O

come, let us a - dore him, ___ Christ, ___ the Lord!

Additional Lyrics

2. Sing choirs of angels, sing in exultation.
   O sing all ye citizens of heaven above.
   Glory to God in the highest.

O Holy Night

English Words by D.S. Dwight
Music by Adolphe Adam

Strum Pattern: 7, 9
Pick Pattern: 7, 9
Verse
Slow and Flowing

1. O Ho - ly night _____ the stars are bright - ly shin - ing, it is the
2. Tru - ly He taught us to love _____ one an - oth - er. His law is

night of the dear Sav - ior's birth. _____ Long lay the world _____ in
love, and His gos - pel is peace. _____ Chains shall He break, for the

sin and er - ror pin - ing, 'til He ap - peared and the soul felt its
slave _____ is our broth - er, and in His name all op - pres - sion shall

worth. _____ A thrill of hope the wear - y soul re -
cease. _____ Sweet hymns of joy in grate - ful cho - rus

joic - es, for yon - der breaks a new and glor - ious morn.
raise we. Let all with - in us praise His ho - ly name.

Chorus

Am ... Em ... Dm

Fall _____ on your knees, _____ oh, hear _____ the an - gel
Christ _____ is the Lord, _____ oh, praise _____ His name for -

Am ... C ... G7 ... C ... F

voic - es! O night _____ di - vine, _____ O
ev - er! His pow'r _____ and glo - ry

C ... G7 ... C ... 1. G ... G7

night _____ when Christ was born! _____ O night! _____ O
ev - er - more pro - claim! _____ His

C ... F ... C ... G7 ... C

Ho - ly night! O night di - vine! _____

2. G ... G7 ... C ... F

pow'r _____ and glo - ry _____

C ... G7 ... C

ev - er - more pro - claim. _____

O Come, O Come Immanuel

Plainsong, 13th Century
Words translated by John M. Neale and Henry S. Coffin

Strum Pattern: 4
Pick Pattern: 5

Verse
Slowly And Expressively

1. O come, O come Im-man-u-el, and
2. See Additional Lyrics

ran-som cap-tive Is-ra-el, that mourns in lone-ly

ex-ile here un-til the Son of God _____ ap-

Chorus

pear. Re-joice, re-joice! Im-man-u-

el shall come to thee, O Is-ra-el!

Additional Lyrics

2. O come, Thou Key Of David, come
And open wide our heav'nly home.
Make safe the way that leads on high
And close the path to misery.

O Little Town Of Bethlehem

Words by Phillips Brooks
Music by Lewis H. Redner

Strum Pattern: 4
Pick Pattern: 5

Verse
Quietly

Additional Lyrics

2. For Christ is born of Mary, and gathered all above.
   While mortals sleep the angels keep
   Their watch of wond'ring love.
   O morning stars, together proclaim the holy birth!
   And praises sing to God the King,
   And peace to men on earth!

Parade Of The Wooden Soldiers

English Lyrics by Ballard MacDonald
Music by Leon Jessel

Strum Pattern: 2
Pick Pattern: 3
Verse
March Tempo

Once In Royal David's City

Words by C.F. Alexander
Music by H.J. Gauntlett

Strum Pattern: 4
Pick Pattern: 5

Verse
Quietly

1. Once in roy - al Da - vid's cit - y, stood a low - ly cat - tle __ shed,

where a moth - er laid __ her __ ba - by in a man - ger for __ His __ bed.

Ma - ry was that moth - er mild, Je - sus Christ her lit - tle __ child.

Additional Lyrics

2. And our eyes at last shall see Him,
Through His own redeeming love.
For that child so dear and gentle
Is our Lord in heav'n above.
And He leads His children on
To the place where He is gone.

Pat-A-Pan

Words and Music by Bernard de la Monnoye

Strum Pattern: 2, 3
Pick Pattern: 2, 3

Verse
Very Fast

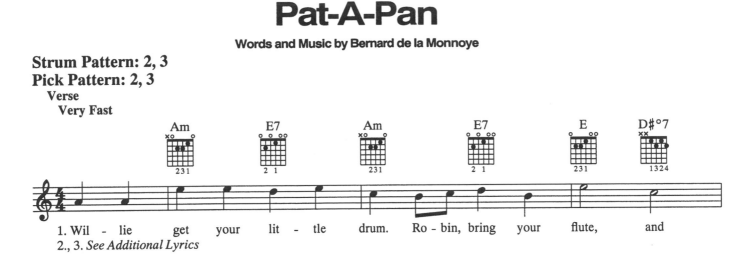

1. Wil - lie get your lit - tle drum. Ro - bin, bring your flute, and
2., 3. *See Additional Lyrics*

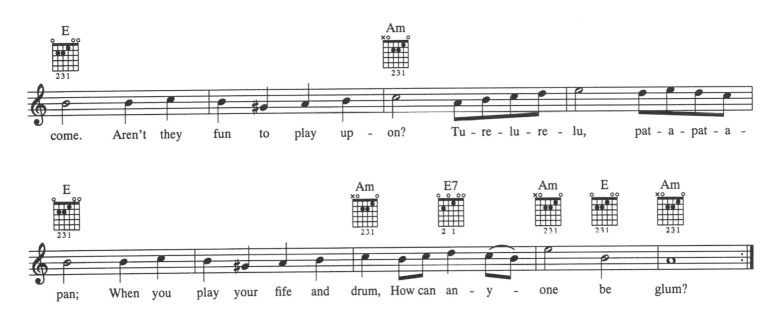

come. Aren't they fun to play up - on? Tu - re - lu - re - lu, pat - a - pat - a -

pan; When you play your fife and drum, How can an - y - one be glum?

Additional Lyrics

2. When the men of olden days
   Gave the King of Kings their praise,
   They had pipes to play upon.
   Tu-re-lu-re-lu, pat-a-pat-a-pan.
   And also the drums they'd play.
   Full of joy, on Christmas Day.

3. God and man today become
   Closely joined as flute and drum.
   Let the joyous tune play on!
   Tu-re-lu-re-lu, pat-a-pat-a-pan.
   As the instruments you play,
   We will sing, this Christmas Day.

Pretty Paper

Words and Music by Willie Nelson

Strum Pattern: 8, 7
Pick Pattern: 8, 9

Verse
Slowly, With Expression

1. Crowd - ed streets, bus - y feet hus - tle by him. _____ Down - town shop - pers, Christ - mas is nigh. _____ There he sits all a - lone on the side - walk. _____ Hop - ing that you won't pass him by. _____ 2. Should you stop; bet - ter not, much too bus - y. _____ You're in a hur - ry, my how time does fly. _____ In the dis - tance the ring - ing of ___ laugh - ter _____ and in the midst of the laugh - ter he cries. _____ Pret - ty

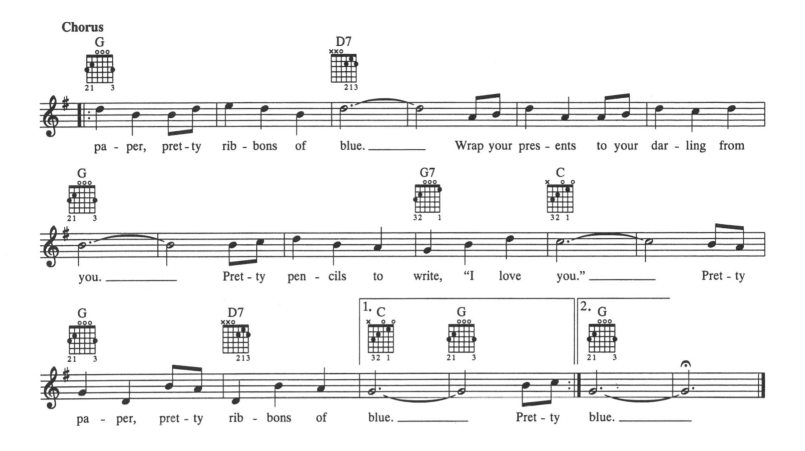

pa - per, pretty rib - bons of blue._____ Wrap your pres - ents to your dar - ling from

you._____ Pretty pen - cils to write, "I love you." _____ Pretty

pa - per, pret - ty rib - bons of blue. _____ Pretty blue. _____

A Child Is Born In Bethlehem

Traditional

Strum Pattern: 4
Pick Pattern: 3

Verse
Moderately

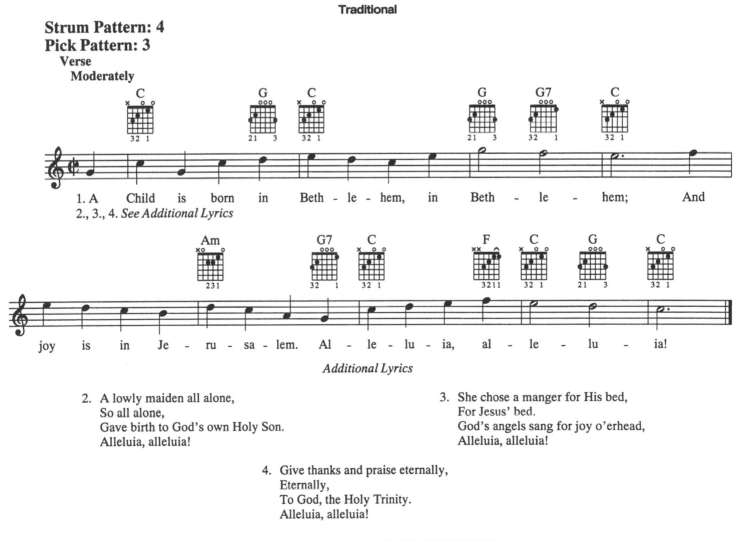

1. A Child is born in Beth - le - hem, in Beth - le - hem; And
2., 3., 4. *See Additional Lyrics*

joy is in Je - ru - sa - lem. Al - le - lu - ia, al - le - lu - ia!

Additional Lyrics

2. A lowly maiden all alone,
   So all alone,
   Gave birth to God's own Holy Son.
   Alleluia, alleluia!

3. She chose a manger for His bed,
   For Jesus' bed.
   God's angels sang for joy o'erhead,
   Alleluia, alleluia!

4. Give thanks and praise eternally,
   Eternally,
   To God, the Holy Trinity.
   Alleluia, alleluia!

Rockin' Around The Christmas Tree

Music and Lyrics by Johnny Marks

Strum Pattern: 2, 6
Pick Pattern: 4, 6

Verse
Moderate Rock

1. Rock-in' a - round the Christ - mas tree at the Christ - mas par - ty hop.

Mis - tle - toe hung where you can see ev - 'ry cou - ple tries to stop.

Rock-in' a - round the Christ - mas tree, let the Christ - mas spir - it ring.

La - ter we'll have some pump - kin pie and we'll do some car - ol - ing.

Bridge

You will get a sen - ti - men - tal feel - ing when you hear

voic - es sing - ing, "Let's be jol - ly. Deck the halls with boughs of hol - ly."

I Saw Three Ships

English

Strum Pattern: 8, 7
Pick Pattern: 8, 9

Verse
Spirited

2. Rock-in' a - round the Christ-mas tree, have a hap-py hol-i - day. Ev-'ry-one danc-ing

mer - ri - ly in the new old fash-ioned way. new old fash - ioned way. _____

1. I saw three ships come sail - ing in, on Christ - mas Day, on Christ - mas Day; I
what was in those ships, all three, on Christ - mas Day, on Christ - mas Day; And

saw three ships come sail - ing in, on Christ - mas Day in the morn - ing. 2. And
what was in those ships, all three, on Christ - mas Day in the morn - ing. 3. The

Verse

Vir - gin Mar - y and Christ were there, on Christ - mas Day, on Christ - mas Day; The

Vir - gin Mar - y and Christ were there, on Christ - mas Day in the morn - ing.

Rudolph The Red-Nosed Reindeer

Music and Lyrics by Johnny Marks

Intro
Freely

You know Dash-er and Danc-er and Pranc-er and Vix-en, Com-et and Cu-pid and Don-ner and Blitz-en, but do you re-call the most fa-mous rein-deer of all.

Strum Pattern: 2, 3
Pick Pattern: 2, 3

Verse
Lightly

Ru-dolph, the red-nosed rein-deer had a ver-y shin-y nose, and if you ev-er saw it, you would e-ven say it glows.

All of the oth-er rein-deer used to laugh and call him names,

they nev - er let poor Ru - dolph join in an - y rein - deer games.

Bridge

Then one fog - gy Christ - mas Eve, San - ta came to say,

"Ru - dolph, with your nose so bright, won't you guide my sleigh to - night?" —

Verse

Then how the rein - deer loved him as they shout - ed out with glee;

1.

"Ru - dolph, the red - nosed rein - deer, you'll go down in his - to - ry!"

2.

you'll go down in his - to - ry!" _____

Rise Up, Shepherd, And Follow

Traditional Spiritual

Silent Night

Words by Joseph Mohr
Music by Franz Gruber

Strum Pattern: 7
Pick Pattern: 9

Additional Lyrics

2. Silent night, holy night!
   Shepherds quake at the sight.
   Glories stream from heaven afar.
   Heavenly hosts sing Alleluia.
   Christ the Savior is born!
   Christ the Savior is born!

3. Silent night, holy night!
   Son of God, love's pure light.
   Radiant beams from thy holy face
   With the dawn of redeeming grace,
   Jesus Lord at Thy birth.
   Jesus Lord at Thy birth.

Silver And Gold

Music and Lyrics by Johnny Marks

Strum Pattern: 8
Pick Pattern: 8

Verse
Slowly And Expressively

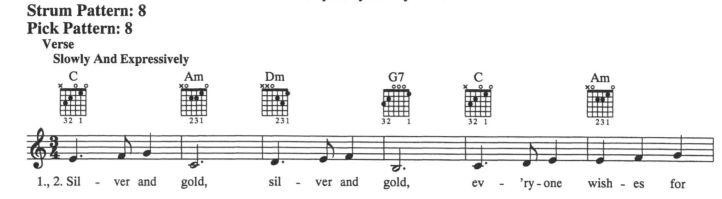

1., 2. Sil - ver and gold, sil - ver and gold, ev - 'ry-one wish - es for

sil - ver and gold. How do you meas - ure its worth, _____

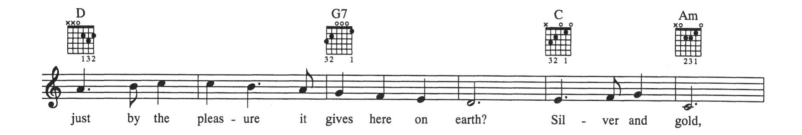

just by the pleas - ure it gives here on earth? Sil - ver and gold,

sil - ver and gold, mean so much more when I see _____ sli - ver and

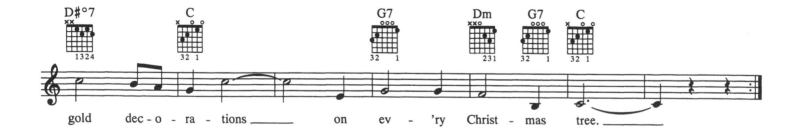

gold dec - o - ra - tions _____ on ev - 'ry Christ - mas tree. _____

Silver Bells

Words and Music by Jay Livingston and Ray Evans

Strum Pattern: 9
Pick Pattern: 8

Additional Lyrics

2. Strings of street lights, even stop lights
   Blink a bright red and green,
   As the shoppers rush home with their treasures.
   Hear the snow crunch, see the kids bunch,
   This is Santa's big scene,
   And above all the bustle you hear:

The Simple Birth

Traditional Flemish

Strum Pattern: 8
Pick Pattern: 8

Verse
Moderately Slow

1. From heav'n there came to earth a ba-by so small: From
2.-5. *See Additional Lyrics*

heav'n there came to earth a ba-by so small:

Chorus

Je-sus, who came for the sake of us all.

Je-sus, who came for the sake of us all.

Additional Lyrics

2. Beneath His tiny head no pillow but hay:
   Beneath His tiny head no pillow but hay:
   God's richest treasures in rude manger lay.
   God's richest treasures in rude manger lay.

3. His eyes of blackest jet were sparkling with light:
   His eyes of blackest jet were sparkling with light:
   Rosy cheeks bloomed on His face fair and bright.
   Rosy cheeks bloomed on His face fair and bright.

4. And from His lovely mouth, the laughter did swell:
   And from His lovely mouth, the laughter did swell:
   When He saw Mary, whom He loved so well.
   When He saw Mary, whom He loved so well.

5. He came to weary earth, so dark and so drear:
   He came to weary earth, so dark and so drear:
   To wish to mankind a blessed New Year.
   To wish to mankind a blessed New Year.

The Snow Lay On The Ground

Traditional

Strum Pattern: 7
Pick Pattern: 9

Verse
Slowly

(Guitar chord diagrams: G, D7, G, D)

1. The snow lay on the ground, the star shone bright when
2., 3. *See Additional Lyrics*

(Guitar chord diagrams: D7, G, D7, G)

Christ our Lord was born on Christ - mas night. Ve - ni - te ad - o -

(Guitar chord diagrams: D7, G, D, D7)

re - mus Do - mi - num; Ve - ni - te ad - o - re - mus

Refrain

(Guitar chord diagrams: G, D, G, G, Am, E)

Do - mi - num. Ve - ni - te ad - o - re - mus Do - mi -

(Guitar chord diagrams: Am, D7, G, D7, G)

num; Ve - ni - te ad - o - re - mus Do - mi - num.

Additional Lyrics

2. 'Twas Mary, virgin pure of Holy Anne
   That brought into this world the God made man.
   She laid him in a stall at Bethlehem.
   The ass and oxen share the roof with them.

3. Saint Joseph too, was by to tend the Child,
   To guard him and protect his mother mild.
   The angels hovered 'round and sang this song;
   Venite adoremus Dominum.

The Star Of Christmas Morning

Traditional

Star Of The East

Words by George Cooper
Music by Amanda Kennedy

Strum Pattern: 9
Pick Pattern: 9

Verse
Joyfully

Suzy Snowflake

Words and Music by Sid Tepper and Roy Bennett

Strum Pattern: 3
Pick Pattern: 3

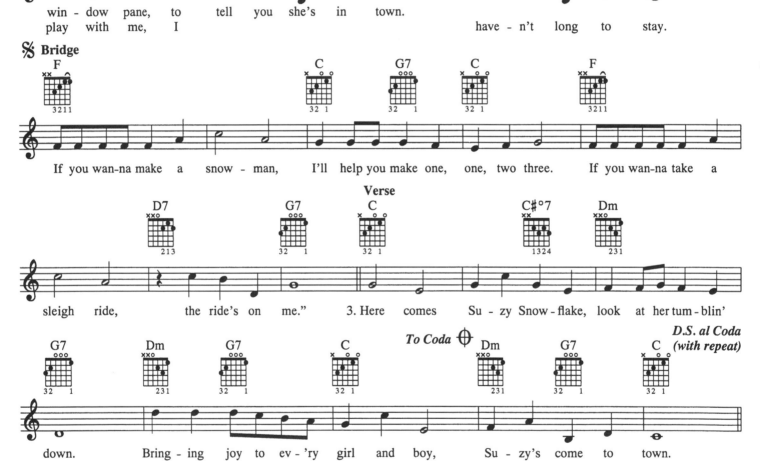

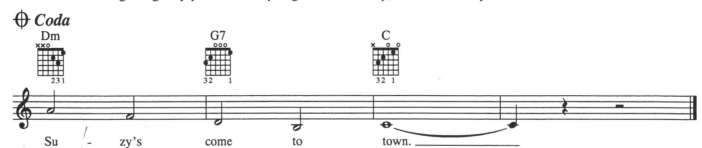

There's A Song In The Air

Words and Music by Josiah G. Holland and Karl P. Harrington

Strum Pattern: 8
Pick Pattern: 8

Verse
Moderately Fast

Additional Lyrics

2. There's a tumult of joy o'er the wonderful birth,
   For the Virgin's sweet boy is the lord of the earth.
   Ay! The star rains its fire while the beautiful sing,
   For the manger of Bethlchem cradles a King!

3. In the light of that star lie the ages impearled,
   And that song from afar has swept over the world.
   Ev'ry hearth is a flame and the beautiful sing
   In the homes of the nations that Jesus is King!

4. We rejoice in the light and we echo the song
   That comes down thro' the night from the heavenly throng.
   Ay! we should to the lovely Evangel they bring,
   And we greet in his cradle, our Savior and King!

The Twelve Days Of Christmas

Traditional

Strum Pattern: 3
Pick Pattern: 3
Verse
Moderately

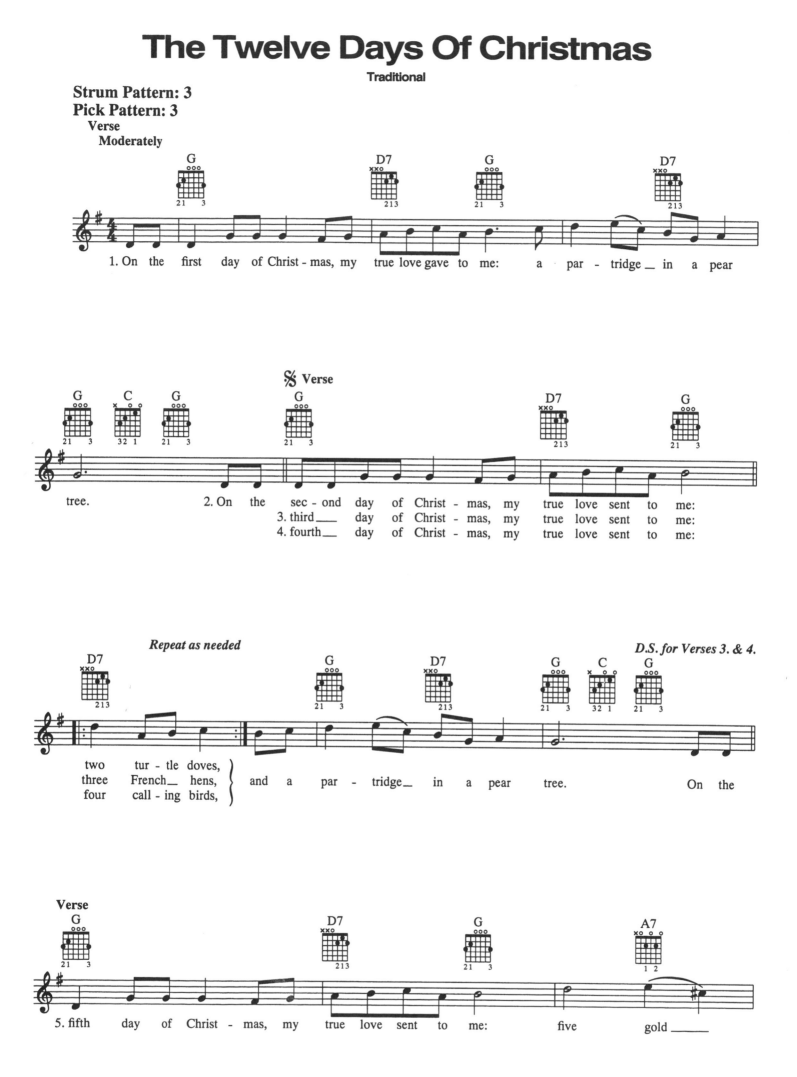

Pick Pattern: 8
Strum Pattern: 8

rings. Four ___ call - ing birds, three French hens,

Pick Pattern: 3
Strum Pattern: 3

12th Verse, To Coda ⊕

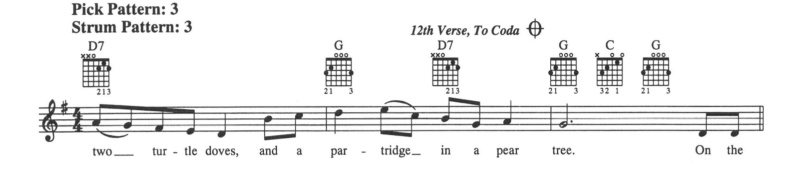

two ___ tur - tle doves, and a par - tridge ___ in a pear tree. On the

Verse

6. sixth ___ day of Christ - mas, my true love sent to me:
7. sev - enth day of Christ - mas, my true love sent to me:
8. eighth ___ day of Christ - mas, my true love sent to me:
9. ninth ___ day of Christ - mas, my true love sent to me:
10. tenth ___ day of Christ - mas, my true love sent to me:
11. 'lev - enth day of Christ - mas, my true love sent to me:
12. twelfth ___ day of Christ - mas, my true love sent to me:

Repeat as needed   *D.S.S. for Veses 7.-12.*   ⊕ *Coda*

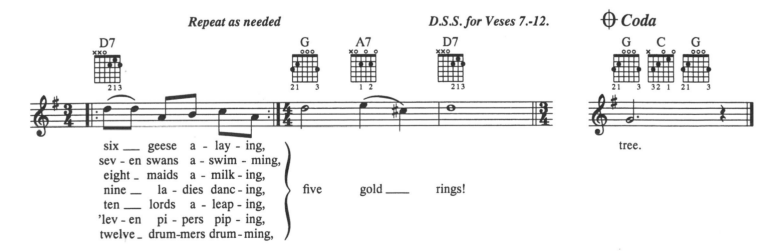

six ___ geese a - lay - ing,
sev - en swans a - swim - ming,
eight ___ maids a - milk - ing,
nine ___ la - dies danc - ing,   } five gold ___ rings!   tree.
ten ___ lords a - leap - ing,
'lev - en pi - pers pip - ing,
twelve ___ drum-mers drum - ming,

'Twas The Night Before Christmas

Words by Clement Clark Moore
Music by F. Henri Klickman

Strum Pattern: 4
Pick Pattern: 5

Verse
Brightly

C   A7   Dm   G7   Dm   G7   C

1. 'Twas the night be-fore Christ-mas, when all through the house, not a crea-ture was stir-ring, not e - ven a mouse. The
2.-7. *See Additional Lyrics*

A7♭5   G   D7   G7

stock-ings were hung by the chim-ney with care, In hopes that Saint Nich-o-las soon would be there. The

C   A7   Dm   G7   Dm   G7   C   C7

chil-dren were nest-led all snug in their beds, while vis-ions of su-gar plums danced through their heads. And

F   A°7   C   Gm6   A7   D7   G7   C

Ma-ma in her 'ker-chief and I in my cap, Had just set-tled our brains for a long win-ter's nap.

Additional Lyrics

2. When out on the lawn there arouse such a clatter;
   I sprang from my bed to see what was the matter.
   Away to the window I flew like a flash,
   Tore open the shutters and threw up the sash.
   The moon, on the breast of the new-fallen snow,
   Gave a lustre of midday to objects below.
   When what to my wondering eyes should appear.
   But a miniature sleigh and eight tiny reindeer.

3. With a little old driver; so lively and quick,
   I knew in a moment it must be Saint Nick.
   More rapid than eagles, his coursers they came
   And he whistled, and shouted, and called them by name;
   "Now, Dasher, Now, Dancer! Now, Prancer! Now, Vixen!
   On Comet! On, Cupid! On Donder and Blitzen!
   To the top of the porch, to the top of the wall!
   Now dash away, dash away, dash away all!"

4. As dry leaves that before the wild hurricane fly,
   When they meet with an obstacle, mount to the sky.
   So up to the house-top the coursers they flew,
   With the sleigh full of toys, and Saint Nicholas, too.
   And then in a twinkling I heard on the roof
   The prancing and pawing of each little hoof.
   As I drew in my head, and was turning around,
   Down the chimney Saint Nicholas came with a bound.

5. He was dressed all in fir from his head to his foot
   And his clothes were all tarnished with ashes and soot.
   And he looked like a peddler just opening his pack.
   His eyes how they twinkled! His dimples how merry!
   His cheeks were like roses, his nose like a cherry,
   His droll little mouth was drawn up like a bow
   And the beard of his chin was as white as the snow.

6. The stump of a pipe he held tight in his teeth
   And the smoke, it encircled his head like a wreath.
   He had a broad face, and a round little belly
   That shook, when he laughed, like a bowl full of jelly.
   He was chubby and plump, a right jolly old elf,
   And I laughed when I saw him, in spite of myself.
   A wink of his eye and a twist of his head,
   Soon gave me to know I had nothing to dread.

7. He spake not a word but went straight to his work,
   And filled all the stockings, then turned with a jerk,
   And laying his finger aside of his nose,
   And giving a nod, up the chimney he rose.
   He sprang to his sleigh, to his team gave a whistle
   And away they all flew like the down of a thistle,
   But I heard him exclaim, ere he drove out of sight:
   "Happy Christmas to all, and all a Good-night!"

Up On The Housetop

Traditional

Strum Pattern: 4, 3
Pick Pattern: 5, 3

Verse
Brightly

1. Up on the house-top rein-deer pause, out jumps good old San-ta Claus.
2. *See Additional Lyrics*

Down thru the chim-ney with lots of toys. All for the lit-tle ones, Christ-mas joys.

Chorus

Ho, ho, ho, who would-n't go? Ho, ho, ho, who would-n't go? ____

Up on the house-top, click, click, click. Down thru the chim-ney with good Saint Nick.

Additional Lyrics

2. First comes the stocking of Little Nell,
   Oh, dear Santa, fill it well.
   Give her a dollie that laughs and cries,
   One that will open and shut her eyes.

We Are Santa's Elves

Music and Lyrics by Johnny Marks

Strum Pattern: 3
Pick Pattern: 3

Additional Lyrics

2. We work hard all day.
   But our work is play.
   Dolls we try out,
   See if they cry out
   We are Santa's elves.

3. Santa knows who's good.
   Do the things you should.
   And we bet you
   He won't forget you.
   We are Santa's elves.

We Three Kings Of Orient Are

Words and Music by John H. Hopkins

Strum Pattern: 8
Pick Pattern: 8

We Wish You A Merry Christmas

Traditional

Strum Pattern: 8, 9
Pick Pattern: 8, 9

Verse
Brightly

1. We wish you a mer-ry Christ-mas, we wish you a mer-ry Christ-mas. We wish you a mer-ry
2. *See Additional Lyrics*

Christ-mas, and a hap-py New Year. Good tid-ings we bring to you and your

kin. Good tid-ings for Christ-mas and a hap-py New Year. 2. We

Year. 3. We wish you a mer-ry Christ-mas. We wish you a mer-ry

Christ-mas. We wish you a mer-ry Christ-mas, and a hap-py New Year.

Additional Lyrics

2. We all know that Santa's coming.
We all know that Santa's coming.
We all know that Santa's coming
And soon will be here.

What Child Is This?

Traditional

Strum Pattern: 8, 7
Pick Pattern: 8, 9

Verse
Slow And Serene

1. What Child is this, ___ who, laid to rest, ___ on Ma - ry's
2. *See Additional Lyrics*

lap ___ is sleep - ing? Whom an - gels greet ___ with an - thems sweet ___ while

shep - herds watch ___ are keep - ing? This, this ___ is Christ the

King, ___ whom shep - herds guard ___ and an - gels sing: Haste,

haste ___ to bring him laud, ___ the Babe, ___ the Son ___ of Ma - ry.

Additional Lyrics

2. So bring Him incense, gold and myrrh,
   Come peasant king to own Him;
   The King of kings salvation brings.
   Let loving hearts enthrone Him,

Chorus Raise, raise the song on high,
   The Virgin sings her lullaby;
   Joy, joy for Christ is born,
   The Babe, the Son of Mary.

Wonderful Christmastime

Words and Music by McCartney

D.C. al Coda

Repeat And Fade

Additional Lyrics

2. The Party's on,
   The feeling's here
   That only comes
   This time of year.

3. The word is out
   About the town,
   To lift a glass.
   Oh, don't look down.

You're All I Want For Christmas

Words and Music by Glen Moore and Seger Ellis

Strum Pattern: 3
Pick Pattern: 5

Verse
Dreamily

MCA music publishing